Praise for *The Fearless Path*:

"Excellent book from a survivor and healer who is setting the world on fire with a fearless path to love, courage and healing."

—Rakesh Samani, Aum Shanti Bookshop owner; New York City

"Because we don't want to deal with negative emotions, we disassociate from the issue at hand. *The Fearless Path* reminds us of a hard truth; we cannot run from our difficult emotions forever, instead we must allow ourselves to heal through reconnecting to our genuine feelings and return to our true self. A wonderful book!"

—Mystic Journey Bookstore, Venice, California

"Leah Guy's book *The Fearless Path* does not offer a 'magic pill' or 'quick fix' for the healing of emotional trauma, rather a guide through strategic exercises to discover your own fearless path uniting Self and Soul utilizing the gentle energetic wisdom of your seven chakras."

—Candace Apple, owner of Phoenix & Dragon Bookstore, Atlanta, Georgia

"Leah applies her upbeat approach to life and intelligent probing into what works in *The Fearless Path*, providing readers with not only a valuable set of personal tools for change, but also hope for a brighter future and a happier life. It is a worthy mission, accomplished nicely by a talented and thoughtful author."

—Chris Kilham, Medicine Hunter

"Leah Guy has reached deep within to discover the truth and now shares that truth with others who are suffering. Her latest book, *The Fearless Path*, truly is a roadmap to liberation that makes emotional healing possible. Leah exposes her wounded self for all to see, then tells what is required to heal from even such a traumatic event as rape. I applaud her on her accomplishments as a writer, spiritual guide, and healer. I can relate to her journey in many ways. Leah Guy's The Fearless Path, and is a journey waiting for you to begin right now."

—Jay Robb, "The Diet Guru," protein powder formulator, and best-selling author of *The Easiest Diet Ever* and *The Fruit Flush 3-Day Detox*

"An inspiring guide to self-acceptance and emotional healing by learning to break the cycle of detachment and take responsibility for your own happiness. An easy and engaging read, this book is a must for anyone who is living in a world of distraction, pain, or fear."

—Summer Auerbach, second generation owner of Rainbow Blossom Natural Food Markets, Louisville, Kentucky

A
Radical Awakening to
Emotional Healing
and
Inner Peace

THE
FEARLESS
PATH

LEAH GUY

New Page BOOKS

THE FEARLESS PATH
EDITED BY GINA SCHENCK
TYPESET BY PERFECTYPE, NASHVILLE, TENN.
Cover design by Howard Grossman
Printed in the U.S.A.

To order this title, please call toll-free 1-800-CAREER-1 (NJ and Canada: 201-848-0310) to order using VISA or MasterCard, or for further information on books from Career Press.

The Career Press, Inc.
12 Parish Drive
Wayne, NJ 07470
www.careerpress.com

Library of Congress Cataloging-in-Publication Data

CIP Data Available Upon Request.

To all who suffer, yet find the courage to love.

ACKNOWLEDGEMENTS

I am extremely grateful for the opportunity to share my voice. My heart is full of love and humility for the time and energy friends and family have given to make this book a reality. My amazing agent and friend John Willig provided encouragement, feedback, and his steadfast presence at every turn. His advice and support have been crucial throughout the process of writing this book. The editors and publishers at New Page are an eager and bright group who are dedicated to bringing wonderful books to the marketplace. Thank you. My mom, Cheryl King, worked tirelessly to read and edit pages for no reason other than she loves me. And thanks to my dad, Rick Guy, who loves and supports me only like an amazing father can.

Clients and personal relationships are my greatest teachers and allow me to put forth my love and healing into the world in a specific way. I'm honored to be with them on their journey. My friend Joan Palmer read and provided feedback and edits with a kind heart and good input. Jim O'Connor offered wisdom, support, and a listening ear throughout the entire process.

A special shout-out of gratitude and love to those who held my hand through the process of this book and throughout my life: Rainer M., Mary

H., Maria M., Gloria T., Paolo C., Laura Z., Helen R., Mackenzie O., Ian O., Tracy S., Becky H., Fred K., Laurie K., Sharon B., Nick S., Tom H., Cindy C., Kevin M., Joe T., Michael L., Michael F., Rob C., and John S. To all my other family and friends who are too many to mention, but vital to my life, thank you!

I am most grateful for the freedom to choose my happiness, my path, and my beliefs. I am free to follow my heart and speak my truth. I am free to pursue dreams and free to say no. I am free to choose God, and to choose love and happiness. It is through the experiences of fear and suffering that provide me the courage to learn and grow. Although there are limits of body, time, and dimension, my Soul is eternally free, and for that, my gratitude is boundless. May faith and grace be an eternal source of freedom for each of us.

CONTENTS

Introduction. 11

Part I: Discover

Chapter 1: Presence 25

Chapter 2: Passion 51

Chapter 3: Devotion 77

Part II: Awaken

Chapter 4: Oasis. 107

Chapter 5: Declare 133

Part III: Transform

Chapter 6: Mystic. 157

Chapter 7: Ascend 183

Conclusion. 207

Index 213

About the Author. 221

More Information. 223

INTRODUCTION

We all experience that one pivotal event. It's the one that takes you to the edge—the one that threatens the solid ground beneath you. There may be more than one life-altering event, but typically one will be the most memorable, the most terrifying, the moment when your Soul calls you to choose life or death. Yes or no. Your response to the call will lay the foundation of how you experience life thereafter.

When I walked into the Birmingham police station 23 years ago I was in shock. Filthy, exhausted, and emotionally paralyzed. I was a shell of a person with only my body in motion. The rest of me was comatose. I remember sitting down in a phone booth to call my parents and tell them what happened. I felt like an actor in a movie. I never believed this could be my life. I never imagined I would make this call. Two nights earlier, I had been raped.

Within 48 hours I changed from being a well-functioning college student with a great part-time job and a rock-star boyfriend to an anxiety-ridden, angry, and depressed individual who felt hopeless and distraught. My world had turned upside down.

Growing up offers plenty of dramatic and difficult life experiences. Mine included anxiety, my parents' divorce, an aunt that was murdered, and later, an eating disorder. Sometimes we put negative life experiences on the back burner so we don't have to deal with our feelings. It may work for a while, but at some point an event will set everything ablaze.

The shame, guilt, and fear raging through my body dominated my sensibilities following the rape. I no longer recognized my young and precious self. Was this my fault? Did I do something wrong? What happens now? This was my first traumatic event and it brought me to the edge. It took many years and a lot of Soul searching to find my terra firma once again.

I had to face the reality of the assault. It was Halloween. I remember running back to the house where the party was held. I screamed for help. I told whoever was listening that Allen, a manager at my workplace, had forced me into the woods and raped me. The proof was the condition of my devil costume: torn stockings with one leg inside out, a mangled tail, and the wetness of his semen caught in the webbing of my stockings. My hair was matted with dried leaves, and my ribs and groin were bruised. I was taken to a friend's apartment where I slept for two days.

When I finally woke up I had to move forward. I pressed charges with the police. Due to various factors, I didn't get far in court. The court process was severely difficult and I barely had the energy to keep my head up, much less fight a toxic judicial system.

I was afraid and unable to function. I quit school, quit my job, and broke up with my boyfriend. Scared and desperate, I was tormented every day with anxiety and humiliation as I tried to make sense of it all and find my way through the ordeal. With my dignity lost, I packed up my life and went home to Kentucky. I suppose there was a part of me still locked in an evidence box in Alabama. Thank God I still had my Soul. As awful as this was, it was the event that forced me to choose whether to wither or blossom. It would be a defining time that catapulted me into the healer I am today.

Emotional healing is similar to physical healing. Healing needs a safe resting place, few distractions, and a lot of love. When I moved home, my dad checked on me every hour, and in the evenings when he came home from work he would sit next to me on the bed and caress my head. He assured me I would be all right, but we both knew I was in deep turmoil. A part of me wanted out of this life.

At first I followed the conventional means of healing. I tried anti-depressants and talk therapy. I read self-help books and created distractions in my mind. I secretly hoped to be saved by something outside of myself like a prince charming. When it came to love, I had no discernment. I became promiscuous, seeking approval from anyone who could make me feel better. I married a wonderful man only to crush our bond with my emotional wounds. He wasn't enough to heal my pain. Nothing was enough.

I was in a tug of war. It was a war of my Soul versus my humanness. My Soul wanted me to respond to my feelings; my humanness fought for a way out of this pain, out of the world. What could I do to relieve the agony without reliving it time and again? As I slowly paid more attention to what I was feeling versus what I was thinking, I understood the emotional distractions. The raucous nights were attempts to avoid my pain, loneliness, and shame. Each morning I woke up knowing that I was on the wrong path, but the resolve of my spirit was stronger. I no longer cared about the person who accosted me; I just wanted my life back.

The road to healing began with research and exploration of energy healers, shamans, ancient spiritual traditions, and body-mind therapies. Tending to my feelings was a difficult and scary process, but I began to see positive results. Meditation and developing my intuition were aspects of regaining my mental stability and I also began to understand the concept of energy medicine. As the healing transpired, trust and faith reasserted themselves and I was able to listen to the desires of my heart. My healing talents were discovered through the process of being healed. I started connecting to Leah again, and life was beginning to make sense in a beautiful new way.

My journey to wellness began more than 22 years ago, and I continue to incorporate the principles in this book—emotional healing, bodywork, yoga, breath work, organic nutrition, and meditation—into my life and in my healing work with others.

As a healer, I'm afforded the opportunity to help people change and grow. Many people believe healers perform magic. That's far from the truth. Healers, like me, are only the conduit of energy and counsel to help others reach greater heights. I think of it as helping others turn the trans-formational corner.

As I discovered, when we commit to healing, we say yes to growth. We discover that life is actually working for us, not against us.

What Is Emotional Healing?

People are suffering and want to feel better. The suffering is not only from negative emotions, but from suppressing the positive ones as well. *The Fearless Path* is a process that allows your fullest potential of happiness and peace.

At some level, being emotionally unhealthy gets in the way of most any interaction. It's hard to excel in work, focus on a task, or have positive relationships when there is inner turmoil. Life becomes a constant jug-gling act, trying to balance the demands of our lives with the demands of our bodies, minds, and emotions. With the practice of emotional healing, you'll manage your relationships better, be more focused and productive, have a more fulfilling work life, less drama, and the freedom of spirit to achieve your goals.

> Emotional healing is the connection of Self to Soul.

Emotional wellness is just as important as physical wellness and leads to a more satisfying experience of life.

A deep voice within may be alerting you that something is not right, not whole. It speaks in the language of shame, anxiety, fear, or depression and craves the experience of wholeness and connectivity to your Soul. The radical road to self-love is to integrate the past with the reality of your present life without shame or blame. Staying connected is empowering, and where there is power and love, there is action and fearlessness.

Getting past the fear and moving toward healing is tricky because fear is the great emotional chameleon. It morphs into shapes or expressions, masking genuine feelings of excitement, loneliness, hope, sadness, exhilaration, grief, and shame. Regardless of how it presents itself, fear blocks your emotional freedom. You may be a quiet person by nature, or you may have developed the fear to speak because no one listened to you as a child and it crushed your self-confidence. It is fear that keeps you from breaking free of the cycle, fear of not being worthy, heard, or loved.

There are only a few things that we can't control in life, but those few things give us such fear that our whole lives operate in avoidance of them. These include fear of death, rejection, pain, and other people's reactions. Some people also have little hope in their lives for redemption, and find themselves draped in an oppressive cloak of despair.

When trying to deal with negative or difficult emotions in life, people often attempt to detach or break free from the pain. Detachment, however, breaks the connection of Self to Soul, which causes fragmentation in thought, behavior, and authentic emotions. Self is defined differently than Soul, at least for the purposes of this book. Self is your humanness, the grounded and present energy that contains body, mind, and spirit. Soul is the eternal part of who you are, the conductor of your life that inhabits your Self.

As the Self detaches from emotions, it distances from the Soul. This is likely a form of self-preservation directed by our limited minds. Your Soul craves connection and feeling, as emotion is the very essence of its expression. Your Soul gauges and translates experiences through emotion, but we humans run from emotions, especially the bad ones, to avoid pain.

The Fearless Path offers a better approach. The word **healing** means wholeness. To be whole, you mend the broken pieces of your Self back together, not tear them apart. It's about connection rather than separation. The goal is to become fully functioning, whole, and heart-centered individuals who can continue to grow not in spite of the pain, but because of the pain. You must be willing to resist the urge to flee negative emotions or the memory of them and instead learn how to hold them tenderly, with care, compassion, and full acceptance.

The process of healing provides a reconnection of your heart to your spirit, of Self to your Soul. You possess exactly what you need to become self-actualized.

Your life story is unique, as will be your healing. But emotions are universal and relatable. No matter the specific affliction, one can identify a person's struggle with varying degrees of accuracy. You can never totally escape suffering, as suffering is part of life. You can, however, become free from emotional entrapment brought on by disconnection, disassociation, displacement, or detachment. It's not possible to enjoy freedom while resisting pain or denying experiences.

There's no easy escape ladder from your pain. There's no back door for a quick exit. The way to healing is with love. Not possessiveness, but acceptance. Not resentment, but forgiveness. Not detachment, but attachment to Self and Soul. This includes all your experiences over your lifetime as well as the emotions that they provoked. This is the fearless path. This is where love resides. This is how you can attain the radical life of peace.

This book offers more than information about fear or anxiety, but these are common symptoms of what is becoming an epidemic condition I call Post Traumatic Emotional Disorder (PTED). Whereas Post Traumatic

Stress Disorder (PTSD) is a result of severely shocking, dangerous, or scary situations and trauma, PTED can be the result of normal, but severely impactful, life experiences that cause negative or difficult emotions. Those with Post Traumatic Emotional Disorder continue to suffer long after emotional harm or pain is inflicted because they have not learned how to deal with their feelings appropriately. It is possible to learn how to welcome authentic feelings of the present and not react to dramatic triggers of the past through the process of emotional healing.

A major aspect of emotional healing is taking responsibility for your feelings and your happiness. This is not to take responsibility for someone else's issues, but to accept the difficult things in your life and own them as part of your being. It is having the maturity to acknowledge that certain events have shaped your life but don't define your life. Don't try to let go of your past, move forward with it.

There's no finish line to healing. It's a process. In our quick-fix society it's the "process" part that turns people off. The "ing" of healing makes it seem perpetual, and it is. Some people attempt to bypass the whole healing process by calling the doctor for a pill to ease their emotional or mental suffering. I invite you to a richer, more radical life. Healing requires bravery and a new direction. Step into the process of healing and watch your life transform. There is relief available in the midst of

> I am not what happened to me, I am what I choose to become.
> —Carl Jung

the heal(ing) if you learn how to access it. This book offers the tools, insight, and inspiration needed to travel the path to self-love and peace.

It may seem like a big undertaking, but *The Fearless Path* will identify and guide you through difficult emotions and help you deploy strategies to make you stronger, not weaker.

How to Use This Book

This book identifies the primary ways that we become imbalanced in our lives and provides strategies to restore and redeem your emotional health. As you work through the process, the integrity of your mind and spirit will be fortified. One of the ways I began healing and experienced change in my life was to understand the subtle energy system and the pragmatic way it relates to life. You may also benefit from a basic understanding of this age-old wisdom and have the desire to translate the information to your own healing. There is power in knowledge.

Life experiences imprint energetic patterns into our chakras, which are centers within the body where spiritual power and energy flow. As we respond to different life experiences, our body and energy change according to the health of our emotions, our mind, and our habits. The energy of chakras fluctuates, as do the emotions and experiences in our lives. Usually, however, we can notice patterns. Each chakra, or energy center, governs different aspects of our physical, mental, emotional, and spiritual bodies as they work together to create a wholeness and balance in our overall health.

Sometimes the energy contracts, stagnates, or is suppressed. Sometimes the energy is over-charged and misused. There are various physical and emotional effects from each of these different patterns. This book will help you to better understand the patterns that cause blocks, imbalances, and disease, and how patterns can shift to create freedom, self-love, and peace. To help you, each chapter corresponds to the seven major chakras in your body. This is your guide to healing in a more holistic way, through emotion, mind, and energy.

You will also discover how issues such as OCD, eating disorders, obesity, and other maladies emerge due to unprocessed emotions and imbalanced energies. You will learn about healing antidotes for emotional and energetic imbalances including oils, practical exercises, meditations, and

Emotional Workouts. There's no magic wand, although I do love wands! If you do the work, you will make significant steps toward healing.

The nature of healing requires action as well as inspiration. Utilizing the core principle of connection along with the exercises of Spiritual Mapping, meditation, and Emotional Workouts provides a powerful framework to help you. The Emotional Workouts help exercise your emotional body. Learn and incorporate them into your life on a daily or weekly basis. Just as we do physical workouts to keep our body and health in shape, the Emotional Workouts will keep your spirit and emotional body up to par. They are not all emotionally cathartic, however. Some are physical and fun, and others are challenging and thought-provoking, but all are worthwhile.

As you work through the book, I recommend using a separate journal dedicated to your emotional and spiritual growth to record answers to the exercises and save your thoughts and insights. Be mindful as you partici-pate in these or other healthy practices to connect your energy and focus on what you are doing in the moment. Positive intention goes a long way toward healing.

Spiritual Mapping is a tool I created to help find healing and mean-ing between our suffering and the purity of our hearts. To experience radical self-love, you must discover the links between your current reality, including unwanted or distressing emotions, and the desires of your Soul. Somewhere between the two, there is a choice or action that was based in fear. When using this process, you will accept and apply compassion and love to your reality. Spiritual Mapping is not about judgment or blame, nor is it about the law of attraction or a type of magic trick. It's a visible path to track your feelings, choices, and behaviors that have positioned you in a particular moment. Mapping should be applied to self-imposed suffering, not the suffering that is caused by other factors.

Spiritual Mapping allows a new perspective on your life and it requires brutal honesty. Maps can reveal issues like guilt that lead to addiction, or indicate how loneliness is sparked by a deep fear of abandonment. You may be hiding behind a dissatisfying job or stuck in a bad relationship due to choices you made long ago about your worthiness. The map will help you discover that peace and freedom are available to you as you track back to your heart.

At the end of each chapter you will find basic information on each chakra, as well as a meditation to help balance and fortify the corresponding energy center and the mind. Each area has colors, gemstones, and oils that can be used as supplemental tools for balancing and support. However, please note that these are not cures and they should not take the place of emotional and physical self-care.

Color therapy can be used regularly by surrounding yourself with the colors that help correct the energy imbalance. Clothes, foods, and home décor are simple ways to achieve good results. Gemstones are gifts of nature that provide subtle and nurturing energy. The ones listed are popular, as they help to restore balance to each chakra. Gemstones may also aid in the calming or stimulation of our environments. They can be worn as jewelry, kept in a pocket or bag, or placed around your home. Some people like to put stones near their computer or bed, or try them under the pillow or mattress. Essential oils are fragrant essences of plants that can have a therapeutic effect. They absorb into the bloodstream and have an aromatherapy effect on mood and emotions. Essential oils can be strong, so use caution before placing directly on the skin. Use in baths, diffusers, or add to home products like lotions or detergents. I have formulated personal roll-ons to be used as perfume and Chakra Balancing Oils. You can find them on my website. If you need more assistance with Spiritual Mapping, meditation, or any of the supplemental healing tools, please visit *www.ModernSage.com*.

These tools are not to be used to prescribe or diagnose ailments, afflictions, or disease. If you have medical conditions that fall outside the scope of this book, please seek the help of a physician. The recommended healing exercises can be used with positive effect in addition to prescribed medical treatment.

The people and stories in this book are true (with name changes) and are meant to offer inspiration for your personal healing and for the transformation of the collective consciousness. There is relief in knowing we are not alone. I've found peace and balance during personal trials by using the concepts in this book. My life is now free of addictions, cravings, emotional anxiety, and guilt. I'm not perfect, but I feel whole. There's no longer an internal war trying to disconnect me from my pain. I want to help you end the battle as well.

My hope is that this book offers the inspiration you need to ignite radical self-love and find inner peace. There is freedom within. Let's get started.

PART I
Discover

CHAPTER 1

Presence

There is a divine purpose behind everything—
and therefore a divine presence in everything.
—Neale Donald Walsch

Rich was a nice-looking man in his late 40s with a worn face, and a scent of smoke and yesterday's drink. He had been homeless for several years and the street was worn on to his skin. As we sat on the stoop and talked, his mind was sharp and his heart open, eager to tell his story. Rich was an artist and had multiple works displayed in museums around the country. He said when possible he would hitchhike to see his creations to remind himself of who he was. I asked Rich how he ended up on the street. It seemed odd that such a gifted man would be so down and out. Rich said he made some mistakes in life—mistakes that cost him his marriage and later his relationship with his daughter. The pain of losing his family was unbearable. When he lost hope of rekindling the relationships, he lost hope in himself. He turned to alcohol. Days turned into weeks, weeks turned into months as he fell deeper into the abyss, losing focus on his work, on his purpose, and on his Soul. Eventually he was homeless.

As we talked, through tears in our eyes, he realized that love was still alive in his heart. He had much more to offer the world. He wanted to change and live his life with love and freedom. His vulnerability touched my heart. I gave him a big hug and he returned the same.

Several months later I saw Rich on the side of the road walking near one of my favorite grocery stores. He looked nice and clean with a spark in his step. I stopped the car to talk. Rich beamed with pride as he told me about his new job as an in-store artist at the grocery. He had stopped drinking, reached out to his daughter, and rented an apartment. It took bravery to open his heart and trust himself again, but his determination paid off. There was life in his eyes and a hope and happiness that replaced the emptiness and despair of previous months. Rich had truly resurrected himself from the trenches. He has been my inspiration ever since.

Rich's story is a story of redemption, of the phoenix rising, of being born anew from the ashes of self-combustion. It's this kind of possibility and strength that we all desire. Perhaps that's why you're reading this book. You know deep inside that you can rise from your ashes. No matter what your afflictions or mistakes, you seek to resuscitate your heart and find harmony with your Soul. You want more from life than constant suffering. You're searching for the "how" so that you, too, can awaken to self-love and peace.

Most of us have fallen to our knees with heart-strangling emotional pain at some point or another. More common is the day-to-day suffering from anxiety, grief, fear, depression, or low self-worth. The number of people taking drugs to treat psychological or behavioral disorders is staggering. Almost half of the U.S. population suffers from debilitating anxiety or depression. It costs millions in healthcare and lost wages, personal happiness, and, in too many cases, it costs life itself. There is a better way.

To experience healing and happiness is to stay connected to your Soul, your heart, *and* your experiences. By doing this, you become stronger and whole, not living in weakness and fear. Rich made his decision to reconnect to his heart while living on the streets. You can make it from your office or bedroom if you decide that you want to connect to love, to Self, and to life again.

It is your Soul's calling to be alive, to grow, and to feel. There's an innate desire within to stop the torture of self-imposed suffering, or to rise from the ashes when the world has beaten you down. With an intense and poignant purpose, you came into this world with a soaring spirit. That's your true nature. Anything less is learned by the human mind of limited beliefs.

Fear and the Truth in Being Human

We all know fear; what it looks like, feels like, and even what it smells like when it approaches. We believe that fear controls us, but we are the masters of fear. Long before there is valid reason to experience fear, we manufacture it. Beyond the fear of change or of death, many people fear their own feelings, so they try to squelch them. The unsuccessful attempts to suffocate difficult emotions cause distress in all areas of our lives.

Beginning in childhood, we encounter the gnarly tentacles of fear

> We fear violence less than our own feelings. Personal, private, solitary pain is more terrifying than what anyone else can inflict.
> —Jim Morrison

such as abandonment, fear of hunger, of not being loved, of not being good enough, or even fear of the boogey-man. We learn early on what doesn't feel good and then try to avoid experiences that make us feel "not good" again. We then create an invisible cloak of protection to use as an emotional hiding place.

Fear can affect more than your mind. It can dampen your happiness and block the potential of deeper, more authentic living. Its crippling power can stop you in your tracks and convince you to abandon your hopes and dreams. Fear keeps us addicted, isolated, and defeated. It straps us to bad relationships, or keeps us from relationships altogether. It smothers our capacity to love and blocks our true feelings.

People who attend my workshops are often afflicted with common symptoms of emotional dis-ease such as anxiety, loneliness, remorse and grief, phobias, skin conditions, stress, and sleeplessness. Their feelings of being trapped, unhappy, and scared affect every organ in their body.

If you seek a life filled with peace, you must first address the fundamental fear of change. Fear bullies its way in front of most kinds of positive self-transformation. It sees self-growth as an opponent to its brash demands that we stay small and stuck, leading shallow lives. If there's one lesson to be learned it is that fear will battle love at most critical junctures of your life.

Use fear as a guide to healing. Fear is the warning bell that change is needed. And change requires action. It is the messenger of a deeper problem that lurks behind its cloak. There is always an unresolved emotion behind anxiety and fear. It's our job to discover what it is.

Fear is our greatest teacher.

If you doubt how fear is present in your life, consider these possible characteristics.

Self-doubt   Negative self-talk

Anxiety   Feeling trapped

Shyness   Disappointment

Avoidance   Jealousy

Eating disorders   Perfectionism

Addictions   Excuses

Control issues   Feeling stuck

OCD   Isolation

Lack of willpower   Dissatisfaction

Complaining   Panic

Emotional distress presents itself in many forms. If you regularly display any of these symptoms, you may be experiencing latent fear or possibly hiding behind fear as an excuse. There's no judgment; we all do it. The point is to recognize that fear is present and can either stop you in your tracks or propel you forward.

The Root Chakra

The Root Chakra is the 1st Chakra of the energy system and it is located near your pubic bone with a vortex of energy that travels down between your legs, toward the Earth. It is the foundation of all the other chakras, and the proper function-

> The root of all fear is disconnection from Source.

ing of this energy field is vital to good health and mental stability. It is important to get the body balanced and grounded. Energetically, this applies to opening and balancing your Root Chakra. Fear is the emotion that blocks or imbalances the 1st Chakra. The exercises and Emotional Workouts in this chapter help balance this energy center and help you feel more stabilized.

Our universe is based on connectivity, from the principles of gravity, to the sun, stratosphere, and the moist soil under our feet. There is not one system or particle that isn't kept in our universe without some connection to another system or particle. In electrical terms, we speak of connectivity as grounding. To ground is to connect electrical equipment to the Earth by a wire or a conductor. In this way, the Earth serves as a conductor, as a protector, and as a ground—an infinite source that can absorb an unlimited amount of current without changing its potential.

What does it mean to be grounded in your physical body and why is this concept so important to your wellbeing? For the same reason as electricity. You are energy and the Earth grounds you as it does for electricity. Your body needs proper grounding to Earth so you can absorb the constant current (life) that comes at you on a regular basis without it changing your potential or harming you.

When you aren't grounded, you may feel uneasy, unstable, or over-reactive. It may feel like you don't belong. This is because you are not tapped into the stabilizing energy of the Earth and it makes you feel disconnected. If you think of the Earth as a source of denser physical energy and the sky or Heavens as a source of lighter spiritual energy, you can see that staying balanced would require being equally connected to both.

This earthly connection is often underrated because so many people try desperately to alleviate their human suffering by means of spiritual elevation, through enlightenment and meditation. But getting fully rooted into your physical being is just as important on the quest to awakening and self-realization.

Being grounded is not the same as being stuck. The essence of the Root energy steadies one's emotions, elicits confidence, creates balance, and in general gives you the anchor to help you to feel stable. With a strong foundation, you can reach higher and meet your full potential. This is where Soul meets world. Where nature meets emotion.

The following list contains some of the physical symptoms you may experience if you are ungrounded or have an imbalance in your Root Chakra. Mark the ones you experience most often.

Constipation	Colitis
Leg weakness	Impotence
Restlessness	Lack of focus
Inability to finish a task	Issues with reproductive organs
Sciatica	Instability

Various issues can make us feel or be ungrounded. Here are a few of the most common.

Sexual abuse

Verbal abuse

Feeling unwanted as a child

Excessive meditation

No stable home or school environment growing up

Being an air sign in astrology

Lack of physical care, exercise

Lack of physical contact as a child or adult

Excessive worry or over-thinking

Selfish or narcissistic personality

Lack of connection to groups, organizations, nature, or the collective consciousness.

There are also emotional symptoms of an imbalance in the Root energy system. These may include one or more from the following list.

Anxiety	Mentally flighty
Feeling insecure	Desire to hide, be a wallflower
Co-dependency	Fear
Not feeling at home	Depression

You don't wake up one day with anxiety. Grief doesn't fall into your heart for no reason. There are many factors in maintaining internal balance and order, and it's important to pay attention to the signs and symptoms that tell us something is wrong. Whether it's a physical, mental, or an emotional issue, addressing the underlying cause is necessary for healing. Our culture supports the treatment of emotional distress with drugs, but if drugs were effective for the majority, there would be more positive results. Instead, we see more angst, violence, obesity, emotional turmoil, addiction, disease, and spiritual separation. These side effects add to the duress while ignoring the underlying nature of our problems.

There's a foundation to being human and it is called *presence*. We are here and present in various ways including physically, spiritually, emotionally, and energetically. It may sound silly, but many people don't understand how important it is to be fully present in their bodies. We forget the preciousness of the moment, the here and now. We take for granted the nature of our bodies, the differentiating aspect of our Souls, and how to live from the presence of our being.

There's a saying: "We're spiritual beings having a human experience." And although that is true, we shouldn't use it as an escape from our human suffering. The suffering in our life provides valuable lessons for the growth of our minds and spirits. These lessons are opportunities to heal. How can our hearts and minds learn in life if we dismiss the lesson that the world provides?

When the roots are deep, greater heights can be achieved.

We are here in human form for a purpose. Our Souls chose to be here. We are beings with great aptitude for learning, loving, and spiritual evolution, but we are also thick masses of energy containing tissue, bones, skin, fat, and fluids that have real physical needs and desire for attention. The first step to emotional healing is to get into your body. Connect to it and be fully present. Put your feet on the ground and feel what nature offers you.

Think of a tree. Trees are strong, sturdy, and tall, with flexible limbs and fragile leaves. The strength and size of the tree starts in its roots. If a tree has a weak root system, it cannot flourish or reach its greatest potential. If you don't feel strong enough to endure a storm it's very possible that some experience or fear has caused you to uproot, sending you the message to pay attention to grounding.

Growing up, it is rare that someone teaches you how to grow strong emotionally when you leave home and face the world. You just wake up one morning and face the rest of your life. It's a struggle to find attachment or connection to anything real. But fear comes from the lack of connection to Self, not connection from others. Luckily, this connection can be developed anywhere, any time.

Lack of connection often stems from lack of trust in Self. We often depend on others for our happiness, entertainment, resources and love, and we forget that we can provide everything that we need. It takes practice to trust yourself and discover ways in which you can be your greatest resource. You may need to make time for personal dates or set small goals to assure your Self that you can, and will, care for all your needs.

In your journal, list three things for which you rely on others. These may be things you don't enjoy, things that frighten you, or things you don't believe you can handle. It could be as simple as taking out the trash or flying solo to Brazil. It is the actions that make you think, "I just can't!"

The more you heal emotionally, the more it's possible to step out of your self-imposed boundary zone and rely on yourself. You don't have to do everything on your own to prove that you're strong, but don't try to escape your potential by passing things off to others.

We idolize heroes because they seem super-human. The truth is heroes are ordinary people with a great sense of purpose, commitment, and determination to respond to the requirements of life. They are generally grounded and connected to Self as well as connected to a cause. They respond to the call without letting the mind or fear guide them down another path. They are connected to the present. They are present. It's simple, yet many people dwell in despair and fear, making it impossible to serve others because they are not capable of saving themselves.

Living in an altered state of consciousness or detached from reality is not the path to healing. We can't resolve disagreements with our loved ones if we are absent in body or mind. We can't serve humanity if we are physically removed from society. We can, however, reap rich personal rewards through meditation, visualizations, energy healing, and prayer, but there are certain Soul lessons that require our feet on the ground and our presence.

Fearless living begins with learning how to create a solid anchor within—to get rooted and grounded, capable to endure life's journey; a journey that can happen in your hometown or in a country far away. No matter where you may be, it's possible to connect into your root. With proper anchoring, you can reach your Soul purpose and experience a new kind of peace.

Emotional Workout

Feet to Earth Grounding Exercise: Preferably without shoes or socks, put your feet to the Earth. It's that simple. Let the soles of your feet connect with the dirt, sand, grass, rock, or in Earth's waters. Take a walk or wade and shuffle, but put your feet to the Earth at least five minutes a day. In the winter, putting your feet in warm water or near a fire can also provide benefits.

Many therapists, philosophers, and gurus talk about the art of detachment. Detachment and letting go are prominent buzzwords in healing. It's like a one-shot prescriptive to cure all ailments, ill feelings, or issues in life. Just "let it go." I think it is poor advice, to the point of being detrimental to your welfare.

We try to manufacture an environment void of suffering. We use food, alcohol, sex, and pretty shiny things to keep eruptions of negative feelings at bay. These distractions only serve to distance us from ourselves. There's no healing in separation. Disconnection is not the way. It only shreds our spirits and hearts. Distractions not only block the negative emotions, but the positive ones as well. Essential emotions of life are part of our nature, and meant to be experienced and incorporated, not discarded. It's the complexity of emotion that allows us to exceed the intelligence of our rational minds.

The theory of "letting go" is essentially a deserted, empty path unless you plan to live a solitary life off the grid. The pretense is that letting go is a simple decision and all your worries and pains will fade away into the unknown cosmic trash can. The truth is that letting go is a path to isolation and disconnection, giving all your power to something or someone of the past. It implies that "You still have me, but I'm trying to get rid of you." The attempt to let go gives as much energy to the source of the pain as it does to the actual work of healing. In fact, it's a vain attempt at trying to release someone else's grasp on you. That's their job. Yours is to process your own emotions and use experiences in your life to continually evolve into your highest nature.

Fear is the guiding force of detachment. Separation is based in fear. We are afraid of being held captive of negative emotions. Dismissing emotions, people, or memory is like removing a body appendage. You may learn to

> Detachment is not the way to happiness.
>
>

adapt, but you will always have the phantom pain. Your connection to Self and your wholeness does not go away with physical removal. Similarly, your emotional wholeness is only damaged by "letting it go." There is no healing or wholeness with damaged, disconnection emotions. Only phantom pain.

Getting rid of an object that an ex gave you doesn't erase the heart-ache over your ex. Don't mistakenly believe that your emotional "stuff" will go to the trash with your physical stuff. If you are bitter about your ex, your focus should be placed on healing the bitterness, not extricating the object. The object only triggers the emotion that needs attention. Later in the chapter, you will read the difference between emotional triggers versus authentic feelings. A cleansing purge of physical items can feel good initially, but it doesn't represent emotional healing.

I recently attended a workshop with a well-known spiritual teacher whose entire teaching was based on the theory of "Let It Go." I looked around the room and saw that no one was being transformed or succeeding with this advice. People were troubled, as if they had tried for years to let go and it didn't get them any closer to happiness or wholeness. In fact, when they asked the teacher how to let go, he was flummoxed. The answer to the question is always some other form of "Let it Go" because the philosophy is a dead end. There is no answer or understanding to this theory, making it a frustrating and useless quest like a cat chasing its tail.

There's a time and place for everything and, in certain circumstances, letting things go (like old smelly socks) is a good idea. It even works in some superficial circumstances of "not sweating the small stuff," such as when a stranger takes your parking spot or when a small infraction is made against you. But real emotional healing does not come from the deficit of disconnection.

I believe attachment, not detachment, is the path to inner peace. Being grounded is essential to physical and emotional health, as is staying connected to the full array of your life experiences. You cannot be emotionally or mentally detached and still be present and whole. Connection is the root of human presence.

Pillar of Strength

Think of a tall, beautiful marble pillar. It's smooth and soft yet incredibly strong. There's something majestic about a solid structure that can withstand the elements of nature as well as be part of nature. Its density makes you feel safe.

Imagine that from the base of your spine to the top of your head you have a marble pillar. This pillar signifies your core, your Soul, your life, and it contains your entire history. Notice what it looks like. Is your pillar skinny or wide? Is it solid or cracked? Is it gray, white, or brown? Get a good image of your inner pillar.

When we try to ignore, deny, or detach pieces of our past from our hearts and minds, it is akin to breaking chunks off our pillar, or at least chipping its beautiful nature. To put those pieces aside or throw them out altogether causes fractured and permanent self-damage. Imagine after each heartache or trauma you broke off pieces from your pillar that corresponded to each hurt. Your pillar would not be strong and beautiful; it would be chipped and fragmented, eventually trying to crumble in its weakness. People try to bash the bad experiences out of their life, only making their pillar more fragile with each attempt. Soon you become unstable, disjointed, or too weak to stand. Is that the way you want your pillar? If you feel weak and cracked and disconnected, it is time to put the pieces of your emotional life back together again.

It's detrimental to continue putting forth so much energy toward letting go of the negative aspects of our lives. The way to healing is to add to the pillar, making it solid and strong. Accepting each part of your past will build your strength, securing your life experiences into your being, and loving every one of them like you would a child. I like to visualize that I have a small worker person inside, patching up my pillar and adding layers with a putty knife each time a blow or hurt comes my way. I've learned if I don't accept my experiences as part of my life, the avoidance of them will take away my strength.

To be a pillar of strength, you must allow and integrate all your history, even the parts you are not proud of or that scare you. It's the accumulation of experiences that makes you whole. To deny any of them makes you broken. It's not the feelings or experience that make you weak; you've already lived through those. It is the fear that the feelings will own us if we don't get them out of our lives. Although the feelings, the memories, and the experiences are what shaped you, they do not have to own you. As you become the leader in your emotional health, you will not need to cower to the fear of emotions. You will accept them and in fact utilize them to strengthen your core, your pillar. Even sensory triggers such as smells, tastes, sounds, or words that you associate with the pain are part of you. To ignore or deny them is to deny a part of your Self. Detachment from who you are causes your spirit to break.

Trauma and heartache can actually set you free. I used a traumatic event as a slingshot to send me on a path much greater than the one I had planned. In my processing, I discovered a deeper part of my self. It was from there that I discovered my healing. Crippled with fear and wailing in agony, my head buried in the dirt and my arms surrendering up to the great unknown, I pled with my Creator to rescue me. I felt a presence on my back and a light in my heart that said "Carry on." From that day forward I have learned how to strengthen my pillar with the experiences of my life.

> Finding inner peace and living from the heart is a radical way to live.

The heavier the weight of suffering, the stronger my pillar shall be built. My heart is lighter with love and acceptance, as I no longer carry the baggage there. It's a road that has led to greater Soul satisfaction than the superficial desires my ego had chased in the past. Let's carry on.

Risk Love

Many of the emotions that you experience in life come from fear of love. Every emotion falls under the energy of fear, or the energy of love. Our limited minds and afflicted hearts often choose fear without consciously knowing it. But the Soul will choose love every time. The good news is that in every moment you have a new opportunity to choose love. It feels risky but it's the only route to freedom. For example, if you have an argument with your spouse, it's easy to close the heart and go into protection mode. The next interaction you have with someone may be short-tempered, harsh, or unkind. What you really feel is scared, hurt, or sad. Love stays open to give and receive and has the capacity to separate then from now.

You don't have to settle for a mediocrity in life or in love. Fear tries to lure us into mediocrity, making us believe the work required to choose love is too difficult. Fear also tells us that to have a rich and vibrant life includes too much turbulence and too many difficult emotions that don't justify the risk of love. The truth is, it is only from processing the difficult emotions that you can have positive experiences that you are seeking. There are techniques, meditations, and Emotional Workouts in this book that will give you the courage to risk love. Doing them may bring up even more temporary fear but that's okay. It's part of getting comfortable with being alone with your thoughts and feelings.

Can you risk love in the face of injustice, pain, guilt, shame, grief, anger, trauma, and all the other forms of suffering? Ego (fear) says no; the Soul says yes. When was the last time you allowed yourself to truly express your emotions? Whether it was grief or anger, deep love or joy? Can you be open to pure passion of life in the heat of a moment? Do you allow hearty laughter as part of your daily routine? Can you say what you mean and mean what you say? These are actions of emotion and freedom that come with an open heart, free of fear.

Try to remember a time when you felt deep love for another. Be it a lover or a pet, recall the moment when your heart opened fully and you knew that you were attached in love to this being. Love is an indescribable feeling. We want to care for our loved ones, please them, and do what we can to make them feel wonderful. We want to protect them and be there in difficult times as well as share amazing life experiences. The safer we feel in love, the deeper our love travels.

Do you feel safe to love yourself? Do you treat yourself with the kind of respect and attention that you would give another with whom you fell in love? You should hold these questions in your mind and heart as you read through this book.

As we begin on the healing journey, ask yourself what self-love looks like to you. Is it a mid-day luxurious bath? Eating high-quality foods? Taking time each day for reflection and self-care? Saying no to offers that aren't good for your spirit? On a piece of paper or in your journal, name three ways that you can experience regular and radical self-love and peace.

By the end of this book I hope you find the courage to incorporate self-love into your daily life. Not as a luxury but as a habit. As we heal, we create space for a new and enriching life. There's nothing selfish about nurturing. Full cups have plenty to share. Empty cups have nothing to give.

Grasping

Grasping is not the same as connecting. We can develop a problem of grasping in fear of losing something. We grasp on to a person who is not suited for us because we fear being alone. We grasp on to jobs because we don't trust the right opportunity is behind door number two. We grasp for experiences and drama so that we feel something as opposed to the mundane existence we face without it. We grasp for attention, fame, or recognition.

Grasping is a fear mechanism that can distract you from the voice of your heart. When we grasp, we are hiding behind the need for connection and the fear that we won't get it. Instead, we take hope that we'll find at least some comfort in what we are clinging to, even if it's not what we really want or need. Perhaps your healing can start here. Not in "letting go" but at the point of the grasp. Look back in your past and see the triggers that sent you into grasping mode. For love, for meaning, for food—what do you grasp out of fear? Take note of three things you've grasped in the last six months.

Although the quick gratification for things we grasp may fill us with a sense of belonging, it usually leads to a new path that is away from our Soul journey. This kind of attachment is not a heart-centered healing attachment. It's a false sense of security born in fear. We can, however, be attached to things with our heart and Soul and be as free as a bird. This is when you know it is a healthy attachment. This is love.

Acceptance

I loved to smoke. I was a full-on addict. I used nicotine to hide emotions, to monitor my weight, to keep me awake, to calm me down, to offset the effects of alcohol, and to keep loneliness at bay. Knowing the dangers, I limited my cigs to just three or four a day. It was moderate usage but I hung on to those smokes like they were life savers. I called them smoky treats.

As I learned to heal, my body and Soul began alerting me that the cigarettes weren't the necessity they used to be. Rather than feeling calm after a smoke, I felt amped up. Smoking wasn't masking my hunger and the nicotine

Acceptance and love transform the heart.

caused more cravings for sugars. I'd wake up shaking and jonesing for a hit. I didn't like to run and hide from people who didn't know I smoked.

I didn't want to be seen. Being a closet smoker was a chore and it was dissatisfying. I remember one night taking a bath and feeling a buzzing sensation at the top of my chest. It was above my heart, what I refer to as the High Heart. Near the thymus gland, my body was talking to me. Physically, I could feel my body buzzing and itching with displeasure from the smoke. Spiritually, I knew I had conflict with the addiction as it wasn't for my highest good. And energetically I felt it no longer matched my vibration. It was like dead weight hanging on to me but I was so afraid of life without my crutch that I kept holding on. The fear kept me addicted for a while longer, but I was running out of excuses. The effort it took to smoke was exhausting and one day I decided to stop. That was it. I no longer smoked and the smoke no longer had me in its grip. It wasn't as hard to quit as I expected. Everything in my body and spirit was done with it. Fear was the only connection. The addiction was no longer a match for me. I didn't need it. I opened myself to a new possibility and that included not smoking.

To deny suffering denies love. The door swings both ways.

The essence of denial is that we don't want to be where we are right now. We don't want the feeling, we don't want the reality, we don't want to change from the comfort we know. Denial is a resistance to change. When I started healing from the rape, I was clinging to things of the past. I didn't want my current life to be real, I wanted it to go away. I was totally ungrounded (rape and physical assault will do that to a person) and I went through a good deal of denial trying to force my life to go back to the way it was before the incident. It was like putting a round peg of the past into a square hole of the present. It didn't fit. The shape of my existence was now contorted and there was no return.

Think of this concept of denial as a new blow-up airbed. When you bought it, the bed fit perfectly in its new box. It was tight, compact, and hard to wrangle out. When you blew it up fully, the air infiltrated every crevice and cranny, making the shape of the airbed change. With more air, it became firmer and more stretched. At this point, it will never be the same shape it was when new, nor can you fit it back into the box. Even if you squeeze and push and flatten with all your might, it just doesn't go in the same as it came out. The structure of the material has been forever changed.

It's the same with healing. You may wrestle with it for a while, but eventually you will either fight with resistance because it is not what you want it to be, or you will give in and allow it to be what it is: a new form that cannot be shoved into its old container. With each experience, your dimension, vibration, and shape are changing and you must not try to crawl back into your former shell. Remember: You are expanding your pillar, not breaking it down.

Many of my clients say they feel stuck, as if trapped in a cage. When people feel trapped they feel the need to trap others. They are mentally trying to break free, but they can't sever the ties to the emotional baggage that has them locked up, much less allow the other person to be set free. They can't fit their lives back into their original packaging so they have no idea where to go or even who they are. They aren't the same shape and they don't understand why their life doesn't seem to fit together. The failed attempts of escape (disconnection) cause a host of new anxieties as they struggle to break free from the past. To be free is to acknowledge and accept what has changed between then and now. Return to the point where you "entered the cage" of your pain and realize that you are different than you were before. The experience has transformed you. When you accept that reality, you can allow self-love and compassion to guide you. You will find that there is no cage.

Part of healing is accepting new energy and emotions that come with happiness and wholeness. We often resist positive feelings as much as the negative ones. We fear freedom because we equate freedom with disconnection. To be free is to be unattached, reckless, flighty, or irresponsible. But it is quite the opposite. The only way we become free is to be attached to our emotions, to be grounded, and to be responsible to our Souls.

Emotional healing helps us achieve a state of tranquility and equanimity that we have not known. As we encounter this state, we must be willing to accept the newness of life that it brings. To accept ourselves fully, we embrace the strength, character, and calmness that develops as a result of allowing love in. As we do this, we awaken to the beauty and connection of the divine. You are divine. Your shame and suffering are the only thing between you and your divine nature, which makes you feel "less than" or incomplete. Accepting the wholeness of who you are allows you to return to your Soul, your divine nature.

As we become present to our emotions and thoughts we become the master of our reality. Actions are determined not only by the mind, but by the spirit. To free yourself from an inner conflict, addiction, or negative habit, listen to all aspects of your being. Become mindful, not just reacting to the mind. What is your body saying to you with physical symptoms as a result of your behavior? Where does your heart alert you that you are grasping? Does your spirit match your actions? Don't just think about the answers to these questions, feel them and write them down.

Feelings vs. Triggers

There's a great difference between authentic feelings and emotional triggers. Healing requires that you distinguish between the two. Triggers are the things that set us off, such as a confrontation, a particular smell, or tone of voice. Triggers provide helpful information, but they are not real feelings. They just bring up the hard edges of your defense. Authentic feelings such as shame, unworthiness, and other emotions will reside in us until we finish processing, at which time they will transform to the next cycle of emotion. Emotions are fluid, ever changing, with each one being unique in texture.

If you confuse a trigger for an emotion you will keep reacting to the past. A trigger is a reminder rather than a return to the negative emotions of a particular event. Triggers become ways to "hang on" to the event, allowing us to respond to them in a similar fashion time and again. If you can separate a feeling from a trigger, you'll find that the way you actually feel right now is quite different than the way the trigger wants you to respond to experiences of the past.

For example, your best friend cheated with your boyfriend. Obviously, it hurt you in a million ways. Ten years later, when you smell her perfume while shopping at a store, you think about what happened. At this point you can respond to the trigger, the perfume, and return to the rage and hurt you felt when your heart was broken. Or you can recognize the trigger for what it is and bring yourself back to the present. In this current moment, you will likely find the truth that you are fine and perhaps you now feel forgiveness and understanding.

Notice the current moment and get specific with the experience of now. It will help you respond to the present instead of react to the past. Focus on your breath. Perhaps your back isn't hurting right now. You have clothes and a roof over your head. You don't feel rage or sadness; you may feel good in this moment. That's the strength in grounding. That's the power of being present. You don't need to emotionally react to every trigger if you honor your true feelings. To catch the trigger and stay present is a challenging practice and requires practice.

When your body is a stable home for your Soul, memories from your past can reside within without causing a reaction to every trigger. This is allowance and acceptance of your past experiences and feelings. You don't have to relive all the events and emotions to heal. Being stuck in the epicenter of trauma or replaying trauma is not the path to healing. Healing comes from allowing and accepting genuine feelings. Emotional triggers then become less dramatic.

Let's Get Physical

When I experience trauma or upset, the first step I take toward emotional healing is to get physical. There's a great deal of healing in physicality. By becoming present and moving your body, eating well, and getting back to basics allows you to regroup and find stability in your foundation.

   After the rape, I moved in with my dad for the summer and took a job remodeling homes. I rode my bike to work each day and went to other people's homes and slammed toilets with hammers, knocked down walls, and scraped paint off old metal fences. I hauled stuff in trucks, hung drywall, and moved one brick at a time from pile to pile. I attribute my sanity to that experience and I believe that the "chop wood, carry water" philosophy is extremely important to achieving wellness. There is great healing in the art of physicality.

> Keeping your body healthy is an expression of gratitude to the whole cosmos—the trees, the clouds, everything.
> —Thich Nhat Han

For just a moment, forget the why, who, when, or how of your emotional distress. Just get your body engaged in the world. Sweat, work, touch the earth, grind it out, and reconnect. The energy that's swirling in your mind, your heart, and your body can start to release with physical motion. It doesn't have to be grunt work. Exercise and play can be just as effective.

Emotional Workout

Balance Nutrition: Stabilization and balance of the body is the key but it is often overlooked in emotional healing. Balanced nutrition is a foundation to self-love and happiness. You may have emotional responses to things like sugars, caffeine, alcohol, dairy, gluten, or soy. Knowing what affects your body and then reducing negative reactions will also help reduce mood swings, anxiety, cravings, insomnia, and nervousness. Balancing blood sugar is vital to stabilizing your emotions. Take good care of your physical temple. When it works in harmony, it eases the processes of the mind and emotions and it is a critical component to healing. Be sure to eat sufficient protein, essential fats, vegetables, and low-sugar fruits. Increase probiotics to support the immune system and eat whole foods from the farm, not a factory.

One of the best things you can do for your Soul is to tend to things of the world and your body. Attention, intention, love, and service are game-changers that will not only ground you, but they will open your heart. Care-tending keeps us connected, attached, and invested to the essence of life. We have an opportunity to be good stewards of our lives, and I believe it is a high responsibility from the Creator. Being a good steward can mean being a good manager, overseer, and supervisor. Caring for things wakes us up to a life beyond our selfish desires. There's always something or someone that needs your care, and the same is true as it relates to your inner world. There is always something inside you that needs your attention. Your inner landscape needs to be tended to—to be heard, to be felt, and to be considered as crucial elements that make up your unique self.

Attachment to things and people creates a gateway to an open heart and a grounded self, providing the foundation for emotional healing. The

> ## Emotional Workout
>
> **Gardening:** Caring for nature and tending to soil is a quick road to grounding and stabilizing the body. Not only does our mind and emotions connect to Mother Nature, but our immune systems and physical health thrive with the micronutrients and probiotics from the soil. Get dirty!

state of non-attachment, being detached, is not what nature intended. Attachment to love leads the way to healing.

As we practice living in the moment, being grounded with full acceptance of what is, we will be prepared to travel greater distances toward our Soul's purpose. When this becomes our path, we are centered, faithful, grounded, and clear. Our Root Chakra is open and connected to the Earth, like a strong tree with healthy limbs flowing with the wind. In the now, we have no anxiety or depression. In the moment, we have freedom.

Blamers and Shamers

There are people who I call blamers and shamers. They are people who can't digest and process negative feelings such as guilt and shame so they transfer those feelings to others. You might think of them as victims. There are also self-shamers—people who harbor shame and guilt to the point of internal combustion. As emotional healers, we own rather than blame. Instead of combusting, we are processing. Instead of blocking experiences, we are inviting them. Regardless of what your history tells you, you do have the choice to choose.

You may be thinking, "Oh, I don't need much healing, I'm over it." But in your mind and heart there is still a twinge of blame from your past that holds you back from the next phase of growth. Maybe you weren't granted the job promotion because you didn't receive the same opportunity as your competitor, so that's your father's fault for not paying for graduate school. You may be "dealing" with it, but at the same time giving in to the belief of "that's just the way things are" so why bother with it anyway? You may have excuses for your failed marriage, your lack of resources, your time accountability, or even your genes. Emotional healing has nothing to do with the offender; it has everything to do with you, the care-taker.

Victims spend a tremendous amount of energy on other people, but in a negative way. They stay stuck in the mire of suffering because they don't use their resources for positive growth and healing. Instead, they give their power away by blaming the world for their troubles. It takes a lot of negative energy to continually find fault for your misery. You can either use the resources that are available to you to blame others, or invest in your personal healing.

Soul Signs are what I call "messages" to pay attention to your Self and do your work. These include feelings of blame, unresolved anger, buried feelings, or general dissatisfaction with life. Being filled with heaviness, chronic anxiety, or sleepless nights are other signs. Soul Signs appear to help you get on a different track. They are like neon road signs telling you to reroute because danger is imminent. If you are unwilling to pay attention to the signs, then your body and mind suffer.

If you want more emotional freedom, take more control. Stop blaming and naming and understand that on your journey to self-realization you are offered nothing but opportunities to grow and evolve. Expansion is not always gentle, but it is Soul-inspired.

Root Chakra Basics

Color: Red

Gemstones: Onyx, Black Obsidian, Hematite, Bloodstone, Tiger's Eye, Black Tourmaline, Jet

Essential Oils: Rosemary, Patchouli, Cinnamon, Cypress, Ylang Ylang, Sandalwood, Vetiver, Clary Sage

Meditation

Sit with closed eyes or find something to focus on. Notice the breath. Inhale and exhale; put your full attention on the breath flowing in and out of your nose. After five to six breaths, take a deep inhale and fully exhale. Now as you breathe try to incorporate this mantra: "I am here." Repeat the simple mantra on your inhale saying "I am" and on the exhale "here." While you sit with the awareness of just being, you may start to notice a thought or emotion. You can stay right here in this moment while also just noticing and being present with whatever thought or feeling bubbles up. Allow it. Watch it, listen to it, and don't judge. Breathing in, "I am" breathing out "here." Stay present with the feeling/thought, not fall victim to it. You can allow it without being overtaken. Try this meditation a few times each week if you're dealing with a trigger or repetitive negative thinking. Remember: The less we resist, the less it persists. This meditation help us come back to the now and be present.

CHAPTER 2

Passion

Pain and suffering are always inevitable for
a large intelligence and a deep heart.
—Fyodor Dostoyevsky

There are two kinds of suffering: the suffering that the world creates for us and the suffering we create ourselves. There's no way around it; suffering is a fundamental part of being human. But you can choose to lessen the suffering and respond to it differently. To lessen suffering, we must change the mindset and actions that help create our problems. To respond differently is to accept the myriad of lessons that suffering provides. If you ignore your feelings and turn away from pain, you will only suffer more.

If we don't grow from suffering, we die from it. Suffering can tether a person to the darker side of life so strongly that it makes passion and the enjoyment of life almost impossible. When you're drowning in the depths of suffering, creativity and your Soul's expression are the last things on your mind.

Suffering is not enjoyable, but it can be another great teacher on your path to healing. It will visit whether it's invited or not. If you are willing to open the door when suffering arrives, you will benefit from its teachings. It can be a catalyst for greater intimacy, creativity, and art. Suffering can bring people and nations together as well as open the heart for deeper compassion and service. To know the pain of suffering is to know the depth of your nature that otherwise would remain buried.

Processing the emotions of suffering allows you to increase trust in yourself and brings you closer to humanity. One can only understand the pain of others by enduring their own. This is not to say you should create unnecessary hardship or dwell in the sea of misery. But creating a new and positive relationship to suffering will help you heal.

Be happy for this moment. This moment is your life.
—Omar Khayyam

There's nothing that can guard you from the perils of this world. Throughout your life, you're subject to pain. But suffering becomes oppressive if you don't learn to accept it and use its presence for spiritual evolution. Blocking negative experiences from our lives does not lead to happiness or good health, but instead it suffocates our spirits.

For at least 10 years I was on the run. Not from the law, but from myself. I was running from my emotions, from pain, from fear. I have a curious spirit and love to explore, but the truth is those years were focused on trying to escape my suffering by creating a new reality. I was hiding. I had experienced anxiety most of my life, the nail-biting, nervous-energy kind. It wasn't until my mid-20s, after the assault, that the anxiety had become an unwanted and yet constant companion. In search of a reprieve, I went back and forth from coast to coast, trying to outrun it. At one point,

I was commuting every six weeks from Louisville to California. Later I would return out West on a quest for my Soul, but Los Angeles was the pit-stop that woke me up to reality.

California was part of my dream as a child. I would go to California and become a star like the fantasy of millions of other 8-year-old kids. My dream was to be on TV, but the truth is Los Angeles became a hiding place for my tainted spirit while I half-heartedly pursued my goals. Being 2,000 miles away from my friends and family allowed me to live my misery in private. The anonymous and huge city supported the toxic waste that was pouring out of my aura. Ultimately it pushed me to the point of a wake-up call.

After the Y2K scare in 2000, I was with my friend Michael driving through Studio City, telling him how my anxiety was becoming unmanageable. I was recovering from a horrific panic episode that happened during my improv class at the Groundlings. The entire class witnessed me freeze, nearly collapse, and be wheeled out by the ambulance. Hours later, with the class on standby,

> Out of suffering have emerged the strongest souls; the most massive characters are seared with scars.
> —Kahlil Gibran

I returned with a clean bill of health. It was "just anxiety." There was no bandage for my embarrassed, ashamed, and fragile spirit. I was so humiliated and scared of a repeat episode that I never went back.

I made excuses for why I was failing to fulfill my dreams in California because to tell the truth about my emotional distress meant that I needed help. I became turned off by Hollywood. I blamed my agent, my lack of resources, and at one point I blamed my hair and dyed it blonde. I tanked major auditions because my confidence was low. My anxiety loop was perpetuated even more by late-night industry parties and a waitressing job that allowed plenty of drinking, smoking, and other unhealthy behaviors. It was impossible to achieve my greatest potential as my emotional life was out of control. I was 27 years old and I felt stuck. I was divorced with no real career. I had not healed from previous traumas. My head told me I should be able to deal with my wretched feelings, but my Soul wasn't settled.

To an outsider, my life looked pretty good. I was chasing my dreams. I wasn't binging or purging, and I was maintaining a relationship with my family. But deep inside I was in pain. I felt like I needed to hide so people wouldn't see how scarred, damaged, and ugly I had become. I couldn't move forward. I wasn't happy and I was trapped in the confines of my sorrows. In the car that day with Michael, I knew I couldn't stay in Los Angeles in my condition. Michael knew it as well, although he was sad to see me go. I needed to leave behind the failed attempt at escape and go somewhere safe to heal.

> One of the biggest contributors of human suffering is disconnection from Self.

You may be familiar with the physical symptoms of anxiety. Your veins rush cold, your bowels loosen, and the world spins. In those moments of panic, you seem to lose control of your life as you know it. Grief creates tightness in your chest and heaviness on your shoulders like a wet blanket of despair. All organs, including your brain and heart, are connected to emotion and spirit. If one system is out of balance, it can throw the other systems out of balance, thus creating discomfort or disease.

The Sacral Chakra

Do you feel lost, anxious, or frightened for your future? Do you procrastinate and find yourself unable to finish a project? Are you bored with life or do you lack direction? If so, you may have blocked energy due to compacted or emotional stagnation. Healing work of this type revolves around the second main energy center called the Sacral Chakra. This is otherwise called the "Feeling Center" and the vortex of its energy is located between the belly button and the pelvis. It's above the Root Chakra (Chapter 1) and works with the Root energy to govern the more carnal desires such as sex and intimacy, relationships, emotions, and creativity. The life you hope to create starts in the Feeling Center, the Sacral Chakra.

The Feeling Center is an area in your body and energy system that processes and feels a lot of emotion. Therefore, it is an area that is prone to unhealthy functioning by blocking our feelings and becoming imbalanced. There are numerous reasons that we get blocked and try to shut down our feelings, but suffering, particularly from guilt, is one of the most common.

For example, if you can't accept and assimilate emotions, you may have trouble digesting food. Stopping the flow of feelings or denying your current reality in hopes of a better one causes more disconnection. Excess worry may cause headaches. Heartbreak can lead to angina. These are not trivial coincidences, but communicable reactions from emotion to body, mind to energy, Soul to Self.

I believe every experience can either be a lesson or it can take you down. It's your choice. When you find yourself in the center of the storm it's difficult to make the correct emotional response. That's why being prepared is crucial. Preparation is achieved through daily practices such as mindfulness, meditation, and physical and Emotional Workouts. These techniques strengthen your core, your pillar, and lead you on the path to healing. You can

> I'm not afraid of storms for I'm learning to sail my ship.
> —Louisa May Alcott

experience radical self-love and freedom from constant suffering. Becoming more centered and grounded provides the foundation that will allow you to go deeper within to meet your true nature. Fear of your feelings is a distraction from doing the work of the Soul.

Every energetic imbalance of the mind, emotions, or spirit presents itself, in due time, as a physical imbalance. Fear keeps people disconnected from their feelings. We're afraid of hurt, abandonment, love, suffering, and death. Afflictions to the spirit such as sexual, emotional, or verbal abuse also create blocks in this area.

Many factors can cause a person to go into protection mode. We subconsciously or consciously shut down the Feeling Center so we are not as susceptible to more negative emotions, but this can trigger physical and emotional ramifications. Physically we see results of blocked energy in the lower abdomen region.

Stagnant energy in the Sacral Chakra can present physical symptoms such as:

Bloating	Tightness in the hips
Urinary or kidney problems	Problems with reproductive organs
Excess fat	Fibroids
Lower abdomen protrusion	Abnormal bowel function
Widening of the hips	Adrenal fatigue
Sore lower back	Lymphatic issues
Fluid retention	Lack of libido

Women tend to process emotions differently than men; therefore, they respond differently to emotional stressors. Women also have the unique connection to carrying and birthing a child, which is at the heart of this energy center. Therefore, women learn to nurture in a different fashion than men. Men can experience problems in this area as well, but men often carry blockages in another energy system, which we'll discuss in Chapter 3.

A weak or blocked Sacral Chakra may express an imbalance of emotional symptoms, which are indicated in the following list.

Feeling detached	Depression
Lack of libido	Codependency
Low self-esteem	Sexual obsession
Lack of creativity	Stuck in a mood or feeling
Intimacy issues	Addiction to food or sex
Jealousy	Fear

Although we all experience some of these symptoms at various times, it's likely that repressed emotions are the cause of recurring symptoms. Attention is needed to free them. If you have on-going physical symptoms, please seek the advice of a physician.

The Emotional Workouts in this chapter will help you begin opening the channels that correspond to Sacral health and free the suffering that is blocking the flow of dynamic, creative, and passionate energy. In general, the goal is to become more flexible in life.

Guilt

Although suffering is often caused by outside influences, it may be surprising to learn that much of our suffering is self-induced by emotions like guilt, shame, and manufactured fear. As it relates to the energy of our health in the 2nd Chakra, the main culprit of imbalances is personal guilt. The weight of guilt is like carrying a bowling ball tied around your waist.

Guilt is a common issue in our society. Guilt makes us believe we are wrong, but guilt never tells both sides of the story. Because we're not taught how to express our true emotions in a healthy way, we tend to internalize and convert authentic feelings such as rage, anger, hurt, or sadness into self-blame, guilt, or shame. Even for those without a guilty conscious, guilt is ingrained in our psyche. We are constantly monitoring our actions and feelings to ascertain our role and responsibility to life. We view the function and dysfunction of our experiences along with the reactions and responses from others. Some people detach from guilt because they cannot handle the emotional weight and feelings that it brings, whether the guilt is warranted or not. This may occur with people who have personality disorders such as narcissism or people who experience a tremendous amount of emotional abuse as a child. In this case, a tremendous amount of energy is still expended on guilt, but on the avoidance or denial of it.

We're taught as youngsters to withhold expressions of our true feelings. We may be told to keep our mouths shut or to sweep difficult feelings under a rug. These are unhealthy behaviors that pound down the hurt and pain, making the emotions hard and impacted deep within our bodies. Suffering then becomes denser and less accessible.

When emotions are pushed deep down and become hardened in our system, it's helpful to work with an energy healer to break up the stagnant and compacted energy. When I work with clients who are suffering from deep impacted emotions in the sacral area, I use a combination of hands-on energy work along with crystals and brass singing bowls. Sound vibrations have a clearing affect in the environment as well as in the body, and they can be a powerful healing tool. Every cell, tissue, and organ in our bodies responds to sound vibration. Utilizing a singing bowl directly on the epicenter of the chakra can have tremendous effect, and the Feeling Center is a wonderful area to begin. As the bowl is played, the vibration and reverberation ripple through the body to soothe the energy and slowly relax and release the blockage.

Paula, a new client, came for a healing session for no reason other than to explore energy healing and to relax. She said she felt fine, maybe a bit anxious from time to time, but overall she was just curious about my work. As we talked, I conducted a quick energy scan with my hands and it was apparent that she was blocked in her sacral area. This is a common area where guilt is stored.

Emotional Workout

Cat-Cow: To free the Feeling Center, get on your hands and knees and make a table top with your back. Place your wrists under your shoulders, knees under your hips. On the inhale, bring your chin to the sky and raise your tailbone up, allowing your belly to dip toward the ground. On the exhale, lower your chin toward your chest as you round your back up, spine toward the ceiling, and tuck the tailbone between your legs. This will massage the spine and open the sacral energy. Repeat five to 10 times per session.

The more I talked with Paula, the more I realized she was suffering. There was another reason for her visit. As in this case, sometimes your Soul will lead you where you need to be without your rational mind knowing.

It can be hard to open up to a stranger and ask for help, but after she sensed my concern, she disclosed her feelings. Paula had suffered for quite some time. Her emotional body was so full of guilt and shame that the energy was palpable. It turned out that she was having health issues in her reproductive organs for many months but was unsuccessful in finding relief or answers. She was also having marital problems and avoiding a confrontation with her husband. Additionally, Paula had tremendous guilt over an abortion that she'd had earlier in life.

It's common for situations like abortion, rape, or abuse to cause an imbalance in the Feeling Center. There is often a significant amount of guilt and shame that accompanies such experiences. Even if a person feels like they made the best decision for their life at the time, there are often difficult emotions buried deep within.

As I worked with Paula, a deep emotional well sprang open within her accompanied by tears and groans of pain. I held her as she writhed and wept. It was the guilt that was keeping her from getting help with her relationship, and this was the most pressing issue causing her suffering. She had spent years trying to disconnect from her guilt, so much so that she became unavailable emotionally for herself or her husband. She couldn't talk with her husband about her needs and his avoidance behavior because she felt so ashamed of her past. Paula didn't feel worthy of his time or love. Paula knew they were capable of a better relationship but she made excuses for them both in order to avoid more pain.

It's not uncommon for one person to make excuses for another so that neither person has to do the work. When neither person communicates or owns responsibility for their behavior and emotions, neither is free of their pain. This behavior makes the other person a silent accomplice to one's suffering, which somehow feels comforting. Paula hid behind her shame to overprotect her husband. His actions were to turn away from intimacy and hide behind his work because he didn't know how to deal with his own issues. Slowly, they moved apart, suffering in silence.

It's also not uncommon to protect the feelings of others. When they inflict pain on us, feelings of low self-worth and lack of self-love can compel us to protect accosters while we carry the blame for the harm they have caused. This is a toxic approach to handling pain. When you can't express your authentic feelings to the person that hurt you, then both of you suffer. Hurt feelings that occur in normal relationships afford us the opportunity to process and heal together.

Shielding your negative emotions from others is evidence of your fear, not your love. This behavior poses as care but it's actually codependency based in shame. Not sharing how you feel is a backdoor approach to control another's experience to protect yourself from their potential response. If coming from a place of love, it is responsible and good to share your authentic feelings with people you love. Share your feelings in a rational and reasonable manner rather than through defense, anger, or accusation.

It's loving and appropriate to allow another person to hear you and to respond with their own choice of actions and feelings. Part of processing emotions is to be present and listen. Don't make excuses for the behaviors of others because you would rather swallow your pain then ask the other person to do their part of the work. You deserve their efforts.

Recently a friend's sister took her own life. Jessica appeared to be an average and healthy 40-year-old, but she was troubled in heart and mind, and was diagnosed with bipolar disorder in recent years. In some ways she was a functional member of society, but she had difficulty keeping her life and rela-

Disconnection from the Soul is the cause of human suffering.

tionships together. Eventually, Jessica drove everyone that cared for her away with her violent threats, rage, and verbal abuse. She lost custody of her daughter, she acquired multiple felony charges, owed money to many businesses, and was in foreclosure on her home. In the face of all her struggles, she refused to take her medicine or accept the help offered by friends and family. She was on a downward spiral of deceit, drugs, and depression, which ultimately ended in suicide.

Although Jessica was unable to carry on relationships of any kind, her family and friends loved her and tried to help. When her family went through her belongings the reality of her passing had set in, along with tremendous guilt. Her brother shared with me that when his mother was alive she always patched up the relationships and problems for his sister, but since his mother's passing four years earlier, his sister had spiraled out of control. He was unable to help her in any way. She wouldn't allow a conversation, much less assistance. She was a tornado of emotional destruction to all that crossed her path.

The brother's wrecked and grief-stricken heart was sinking in deep feelings of guilt. "I feel so guilty. I wish I could go back and fix the relationships and problems for her; maybe she wouldn't have killed herself. Maybe I could have done this for her."

Guilt is common with the loss of a loved one. Throughout the shock and denial stage we go through thoughts of how we could have done more, said more, loved better, forgiven easier. I assured him that even if he could go back and fix everything for her, his intervention wouldn't have changed the outcome, as fixing relationships wasn't the source of the problem. He could not see, much less address, the depth of her agony. Her spirit was injured from certain events in her lifetime.

Unresolved emotional pain along with mental illness kept Jessica from being capable to deal with the vast amount of her suffering. The more she resisted love and aid, the more dramatic her reactions to life became. Her emotional rampages increased with each new incident or loss. No matter how she manipulated situations, she couldn't escape the maze of destruction that she blazed in her path. She refused the prescribed medications as well as the love and assistance that was offered to ease her pain. She could no longer deal with the guilt of her actions, the brokenness of her heart, or the imbalance in her mind.

When the spirit and Soul are connected there's an instinct to survive, a desire to participate in life and achieve personal growth. When spirit and Soul are misaligned due to sickness, emotional barricades, or circumstance, there is a separation or break that has the potential to cause many maladies. Depending on the severity, separation may hinder our ability to maintain relationships or create issues ranging from anxiety to psychosis.

The wound is the place where the light enters you.
—Rumi

Many of us experience injuries to our spirits due to illness, environmental issues, lack of love, or grief. Emotional injuries can make you feel weak, but they can also be the catalyst to build your strength and character. It is right to allow your weakness as it can expand your love and acceptance. This is how you find strength. Avoidance of weakness causes disconnection, which moves us away from our Soul and toward self-inflicted harm, or at the very least, we find ourselves off track from our authentic path.

Emotional Workout

An Exercise on Suffering: Take a piece of blank white paper. Close your eyes and take three deep calming breaths. Open your eyes and write one to two words that capture the essence of your suffering. It may be a name, a disease, an addiction, or a long-harbored feeling of guilt. Don't over-think, just write the first words that come to your mind.

Close your eyes again and envision the word(s) on the page. See the word on the white piece of paper, allowing the word and its feeling to flow into your body with each breath. Repeat the word like a mantra. By doing this, we access and allow the reality of the suffering to re-integrate and become part of our core pillar of strength. This may feel uncomfortable at first, but remain present with it for at least three breaths.

Open your eyes and the turn the paper over. Write a word or two that describes the healing antidote to your suffering. It could be love, forgiveness, a name, an apology, or a feeling such as joy or peace. What is the emotion that is opposite to your suffering?

Close your eyes and take three deep breaths and relax. As you inhale, imagine breathing in this word of healing. Use it as a mantra as you breathe. Inhale the emotion into your being. If you wish, lift the sides of your lips and create a little smile during the process.

Healing happens as we become more present. With our presence, we lose resistance. The less we resist, the less it persists.

As on the paper, the experiences of both suffering and healing exist on the same dimension but from a different perspective. You don't have to sit and only breathe in the suffering, you can go to the other side and breathe in healing. You have the capacity for both. There will always be an equal amount of healing available to mitigate the suffering if you give it the same focus. To discard the suffering, you will also discard the healing antidote as it is attached to the other side of your experience. Healing requires us to suffer. You may think, "If I don't suffer I won't need to heal." But you can't awaken if there's nothing to awaken from. It's the science of polarity. Yin and yang. Good and evil. It's the experience of humanity. Radical self-love awakens as we embrace this reality and integrate the experiences of our suffering so we can transform them into our healing.

Let's pretend your suffering is due to mistrust. Your best friend slept with your spouse, which created serious trust issues. The healing antidote for mistrust is trust. To understand the value of real trust, you will need to understand the depth of mistrust, and unfortunately, this comes from experience. You cannot fully understand the depth of a feeling without the experience. As you suffer mistrust you can experience the healing power of trust. You need the suffering to experience growth. Trust and mistrust live in the same dimension, on the same page, but on opposite sides. You can't experience one without the other. You cannot work with something that doesn't exist.

Soul vs. Spirit

The terms *spirit* and *Soul* are often used interchangeably, being tossed about in the melting pot of spirituality and religion. Although easily confused, the terms are distinctly different.

The spirit is part of your humanness that allows you to communicate with your Creator and your higher self, expressing your spirituality in the world. It's your spirit that understands aspects of life that you can't explain with your human mind. The human spirit is the part of us that understands and connects with your Soul. But your spirit is not your Soul.

Each of us has a unique spirit that manifests itself as character or personality. We use the intelligence of our own spirit to identify another spirit. We often refer to a person's spirit as a dimension of light: "She was such a bright light" or "His spirit just shines." If there is an internal struggle we refer to it as a broken or troubled spirit. Your spirit is affected by the choices you make and how you respond to suffering. Whether we're aware of it or not, the spirit is used in an integral way to understand life. It's the part of us that has a trust in the unknown master plan or divine order that our brains cannot comprehend.

Your Soul is who you are and it never dies. The definition of Soul is the immaterial part of a living being, regarded as immortal. It's also known as your essence. Your Soul is necessary to your being, and the essential nature of your constitution.

Your Soul attempts to guide you through the journey of life, leading with the divine mission of your purpose and heart. Love is born in the Soul. Love transforms but never dies. The Soul does not change or waver like the spirit. It is the handiwork of the Creator of light. You cannot adjust it, improve it, or mend it. It just "is." The Soul is pure, stable, and is the "I am" of who you truly are. To experience harmony and healing you must rediscover your Soul and try to stay in alignment with it as much as possible. Living in accordance with your Soul is to be at peace.

How you communicate and align with your Soul determines how you process fear and love. Choosing fear moves you further away from the desires of your Soul. Choosing love moves you closer to the heart of your Soul. It makes sense that you live a more authentic, happy life as your spirit becomes more aligned with your Soul. This honors your true nature. You gain more ability to digest emotional energies, you have more resources to develop trust, and you achieve a higher perspective to understand suffering. You will also gain more gumption to act on your creative and passionate desires.

Why is it important to live from your Soul? Being aligned with your deepest nature allows authenticity in your actions and reactions. Cultural and societal forces lead you to live a certain way. Perhaps people around you may value money or high-status living, but your Soul may crave simplicity and giving. Your damaged spirit may be happy as a wallflower, but your Soul may have a different desire. Your life path should not be compared with others, or their vision for you. Self-love awakens as you connect to your Soul and live from that authentic place. This is not selfishness. Its life-affirming.

Acting upon the advice of your Soul will take practice. Develop the skills of listening, trust, and action, which we'll explore in chapters 6 and 7. Your Soul communicates with your heart, your mind, and your gut. It's the familiar gut instinct we know, but often ignore. Here are three easy steps to align your Spirit and Soul.

1. Remove distractions: Turn off the television, phone, and computer. Go to a quiet place where you can be alone and comfortable, if only for a short while. Your Soul is waiting for you there. Check in with yourself, your feelings, and your energy. Get centered. Listen deeply, beyond the mind. Listen to your gut.

2. Write: Start free-flow writing in a journal or notebook. Write your thoughts as they emerge until your mind settles. Then keep writing. Your Soul will fall on to these pages, between the lines, in a flash of intuition, a feeling in your gut, or a hope in your heart. This is inspiration. Listen to the soft nudge of encouragement and feel the emotion as you listen. There's a spark inside, full of messages from deep within your Soul. You will feel it as you attune to your inner voice.

3. Take action: Without over-thinking, criticizing, or analyzing, do what your Soul asks you to do. Do it now. If you want

to take piano lessons, call and make an appointment. If you need space from a mediocre relationship, start the discussion. It takes courage to make a change or take the first step. Baby steps are fine, but the time is now. There is no tomorrow, only today. Act on inner desires that are positive, life-enriching, and connected to your authentic Soul.

Digesting Emotional Energies

The gut is an intelligent, interdependent system that controls a portion of our health and how we respond to life. Much of the immune system is housed in the gut. The gut also removes toxic waste that would kill us if left in the body. Information and emotions are also processed in the gut. It's where the lingo "gut instinct" or "follow your gut" originated. The gut and its corresponding energies are smart, as well as creative and passionate. When not in sync with your gut, the source of passion and creativity or the ability to accept intimacy is blocked. This is a signal to unclog the emotional digestive system.

Every organ, tissue, and cell has the capacity to sense feelings as well as the ability to recall moments of pleasure or pain. When you experience a physical ailment like a sore throat or gallbladder attack, you remember what the pain feels like in the location, but you also feel it in your psyche, your cells, and your gut. We are feeling creatures and feelings help us navigate through life. We're either feeling the moment, remembering a feeling, or looking forward to a feeling. It can be problematic if we don't allow the negative feelings to digest completely.

People attempt to stop their feelings before they get too far into their bodies or into their memories. We hope the less time they stay with us, the less impact they will have. It's common to cover the bad feelings with alcohol, sugar, or other numbing agents, and hope that when those wear off, so will the emotion. This doesn't work. Emotions linger until properly handled and processed. If kept at bay, the feelings become old, stale, and rancid, making them hard to digest and leading to a breeding ground for disease.

Think about a food compost. The composted food feeds and nourishes the soil of other plants by utilizing the nutrients from decomposing leftovers. Compost is a tremendous benefit for the growth of the next cycle of foods and plants. Food is alive and continues to provide life when we are finished with it. As we give uneaten food back to nature, insects, worms, and bacteria can decompose the dead matter into nutrients that support living plants. Emotions are the same. Emotions are alive. When we are finished with them, the remaining energy of emotions can be donated back to the emotional cycle rather than discarded. Other parts of our nature then decompose the already-experienced emotion to nurture new emotions and experiences. For example, with time and processing, anger will transform and decompose to become the fertilizer for bliss or sadness. When joy has run its course, it can be decomposed and provide nutrients for impatience or compassion. In this way, we utilize all of our resources as well as expound our emotional intelligence. This is evolution. Our bodies and minds evolve and contribute to the collective consciousness. We should strive to be more emotionally responsible to the expansion of human consciousness as well as our own emotional and spiritual evolvement.

From my childhood until my mid-30s I struggled to digest emotions, especially guilt and shame. I easily absorbed other people's feelings and swallowed my own, which impacted my health in many ways. If someone close to me was nervous, I would feel nervous and wonder what was wrong with me. Many people are highly sensitive and report similar challenges. Emotions can be difficult to sort when personal boundaries are not in place. I lacked the maturity to discuss how I felt, nor could I digest complex feelings at such a young age. I just stuffed them deep inside.

Before the age of 8 I developed a hernia near my groin that required surgery. I was also frequently constipated and bloated along with having pain in my stomach and leg region. This lead to a body image problem. I thought I was too fat, too thick, or too something. Later I realized that fat isn't a feeling. To alleviate my uncomfortable feelings, I relied on distractions such as diet plans, boys, and drama with my friends. When my true emotions surfaced, I had to find another way to deal with my feelings as well as body image issues. The symptoms of emotional pain and energy blocks were apparent.

It took years of trial and error for me to find a better way. With a consistent healthy diet, energy work, and spiritual and emotional healing processes, I worked through the guilt and found clarity about my personal feelings. I no longer absorbed the feelings of others. I still need extra work in this area to stay aware of my emotions, maintain healthy relationships, and continue helping others. The tools in this book continue to help me stay grounded and express my emotions in a healthy way.

I hope you will become an emotional compost. Take time to separate the reactive drama from your real feelings and compost your emotions when possible. All emotions, positive or negative, can be incorporated and composted to fertilize the rest of your experience and growth. As the emotions become richer, so do our lives.

Start by choosing the three emotions that are hardest for you to digest and imagine putting them in your compost. When they present themselves, be reminded that they are the fertilizers for your growth. Churn them and turn them and let them break down. Do not trash or attempt to stop these feelings.

Your gut provides direct clues to how you are responding to life. It's not about grasping in desperation and it's also not about letting go. To grasp is just a form of control that creates a compacted, clogged system. To let go is a self-defeating power struggle. An emotion that is free to be alive will stay as long as it is needed. It will leave when it's ready to transform.

Emotional Workout

Elimination: A healthy digestive system that passes waste with ease is key to being in the flow of life. Be sure to increase probiotics and fermented foods, decrease sugar and processed carbs, and intake more whole foods. Make sure you are having a bowel movement at least once a day and your stools are healthy and complete.

Creativity

Whether you are creative or not, having a clear and well-functioning Feeling Center is crucial to a healthy and vibrant life. The feeling of creative connection is like being plugged into your Soul and all circuits are on. When I sing I feel inspired and free, as if the world is funneling through me. My Soul is happy and my spirit zings. You may experience a similar sensation when you work on a car, help a neighbor, or make a delicious meal. Creativity is a unique expression and none of it is wrong.

> The artist is a receptacle for emotions that come from all over the place: from the sky, from the earth, from a scrap of paper, from a passing shape, from a spider's web.
> —Pablo Picasso

Creativity births ideas, art, design, music, meals, inventions, and books. Creativity plays an important role in healthy relationships, imagination, and how you process information. Open energy channels are vital to fertilize and conceive any type of creativity, so it's important to understand what triggers your passions.

I recently read about a vibrant 90-year-old woman. She's a yoga instructor and a dancer. She's also a mother, wife, entrepreneur, teacher, and sky-diver. In the photo, the light in her eyes dazzled with success and happiness. She lives a full expression of creativity, acting on the desires of her Soul, discovering new interests no matter her age. There are no boundaries or limitations to creativity and passion when your energy flows freely. It's beautiful and magical to witness.

Creativity is an extension of your Soul. When not entrapped in guilt and suffering, it delivers great expression of your being. It inspires moments, sustains relationships, connects with the divine, and translates feelings into self-expression. The more grounded and present you are, the more prolific your creative output.

Emotional Workout

Vision Board: A fast and fun way to connect to your Feeling Center is to create a vision board. Gather various magazines and newspapers, a big piece of poster board, glue, and scissors. Go through magazines and papers and cut out things that look interesting, fun, and desirable or reminds you of you. Find words, colors, images, and shapes. With a creative and uncritical eye, glue them to the board in any pattern that you like. Stay with it until you are satisfied with what you see. You can hang the finished project and use it as a meditation or use it as a reminder of who you are and what you desire. It's a great exercise to reconnect with your Soul's passion. Have fun doing it!

Relationships and Sex

Relationships are hard, but so rewarding. Relationships with lovers, family, friends, or ourselves present similar challenges: to be truthful, to be vulnerable and open-hearted, to choose connection over disconnection. When we become stuck due to a bad relationship, it's a sign that guilt, shame, or mistrust is at play and healing is needed. A good example is a family visit.

How do you feel when you visit relatives you haven't seen in a long time? Do you revert to the behavior of a 10-year-old, reacting to people or situations that push your buttons, or do you stay present, grounded, and centered? As a mature adult, you can be your new and improved self in the face of any trial, including family visits. But it's easy to revert to the way we felt and acted when we were young. These are common signs of long-held emotions that need to be accepted and digested.

Sex is a sacred and beautiful act. Due to the abuse of power and sexual abuse, the sacred act has become a situation to be feared and controlled. The purity of the sex act has become tainted for many people. Additionally, we're taught that only certain desires are normal so we limit the creativity or imagination of what is possible for two lovers to experience, thereby limiting our Sacral energy.

> Used as rocket fuel, sex energy can lift our consciousness to the stars to experience a state of being where love exists in and for itself and has no opposite. On a Soul level, this is our natural state.
> —John Maxwell Taylor

The distrust of sex often begins in childhood. Children have so much to discover about their own feelings, desires, and the functionality of sex, but the mistreatment of sexual energy from others can thwart the early development of a healthy relationship to sexuality. More than we like to admit, children are abused. Sexual exploitation, pornography, trafficking, incest, and molestation are all too common, as is the subtle objectification of our youth. Sexualization and objectification can come from within the family as well as from strangers or society. These multiple layers of toxic energies are difficult to handle, especially for the emotionally immature.

I was a cute child, or so my parents believed, growing up in a middle-class family in an average town. I was often afraid and felt watched. Walking home from elementary school, strangers whistled at me from their cars. Scared, I ran toward the nearest safe house pretending to live there. On random school days, one of my softball coaches would unexpectedly stop by after school when my parents weren't home, standing in the doorway with a flirtatious smile. Luckily I was wise enough to not invite her in. In one way, I felt special for the attention, but on the other hand, it wasn't the kind of attention I wanted. Young girls and boys alike are forced to contend with conflicting emotions of power, guilt in disappointing others, desire, vulnerability, and fear. It's a lot to handle, especially for a child. My experiences made me feel sad, embarrassed, and ashamed. What did I do to invite these strange feelings? Was it my fault? I was conflicted between wanting my outgoing personally to shine yet confused when it would attract unwanted or uncomfortable attention. It takes years of emotional work to learn how to sift through the attractions of others and determine if they are affirming or maligned.

The essence of sexual energy is full of spirit, light, creativity, and freedom, and should not to be feared. It's an energy that can help us harness and manifest some of our fantasies and dreams. We can expand our lives with the dynamic energy of sex if we can allow ourselves to experience vulnerability, intimacy, and trust. The strength of the sacral energy lies in the sacred movement of the Soul,

> Fear is the great enemy of intimacy. Fear makes us run away from each other or cling to each other but does not create true intimacy.
> —Henri Nouwen

flowing freely in the creative balance of masculine and feminine.

How do you become a trusting lover when you've been hurt, taken advantage of, abandoned, abused, or otherwise thrown to the curb? There's a term that I call the "Trusted Nurturer." The Trusted Nurturer is the divine feminine in each of us, man or woman, and it is selfless, giving, and humble. She is powerful, yet open to receive, knowing that her strength is in her weakness. The feminine aspect of each of us understands the need to be nurtured. Her mantra is "As I give, I receive." The Trusted Nurturer has no fear because she provides and enables love, rather than grasping or blocking love. She is the aspects of art and passion, which are fragile yet bold, tender yet strong. She stays connected to heart and Soul while exploring the juicy rivers of life, flowing between uninhibited carnal desires and the spiritual call of the Soul. She brings forth the beauty and presence of sacred intimacy, creating the very trust in herself and her partner. Either or both partners can become the Trusted Nurturer, creating a safe and divine place for the exchange of love. To master this energy is to master the art of passion.

There's no better place than the arms of a lover to practice opening the Feeling Center. Vulnerability, openness, and giving and receiving pleasure and passion helps to enhance the positive flow of energy and the ability to process emotions.

Denying healthy sex is to deny our basic instincts of connection and evolution. Repressed emotions such as anger or distrust can block the energy of sacred intimacy, which is unhealthy. Stifling love and desires in a healthy and consensual way is to block one of the fundamental communications of your Soul.

Freeing the emotional center of your Sacral Chakra, your Feeling Center, will free the passion of your Soul. Work on good functioning of the sexual and elimination organs, physical movement, and developing new bonds of trust and intimacy with loved ones to help restore the integrity and flow of this energy. Processing guilt and shame, and caring for your feelings and relationships will also help to unleash your creativity and well-being.

Emotional Workout

Dance, dance, dance: Music has a powerful effect on the Soul and can awaken the flow of your Feeling Center. Connect to the rhythm and let loose. Sing, dance, and feel the vibe. I do this at home when no one is watching. Dancing has a way of liberating the Soul and it will help you unlock creative energies and ignite your passion. Avoid sideways dancing and put your whole body into the movement. Gyrate, twerk, grind, kick, jump, swirl, and do the crazy man's dance!

Sacral Chakra Basics

Color: Orange

Gemstones: Carnelian, Amber, Coral, Moonstone, Jasper

Essential Oils: Ylang Ylang, Ginger Root, Sandalwood, Orange, Chamomile, Neroli, Jasmine, Lemongrass

Meditation

Close your eyes and focus on the tip of your nose. As you exhale, release the muscles in your forehead, drop your ears and shoulders, and relax your elbows, knees, and toes.

On your next inhale and exhale, incorporate the following mantra: Breathing in. Breathing out. For just a few moments, follow your breath and repeat the mantra to steady your mind and body. Just breathe in and effortlessly let the air flow out of your nostrils. On your next inhale allow the lower stomach muscles to relax, let the sphincter muscle relax, and imagine the channel of energy flowing from the base of your spine up to the top of your head. With each inhale, the tummy, just below the navel, will expand. With each exhale, gently pull the tummy in. Breathing in. Breathing out.

Find a rhythm of breath that feels full but not forced. You may notice that stagnant emotion may start to stir in your belly or well up in your heart as you sit with yourself. This is good. If it is jealousy, allow the jealousy and keep flowing with your breath. Breathing in. Breathing out. Try to bring forth the flip side of jealousy. Breathing In. Breathing Out. Breathe in joy and excitement. Feel the awe of your accomplishments. Try this in the confines of your sacred space. Just breathe, listen, and allow. Breathing in. Breathing out.

CHAPTER 3

Devotion

Love says I am everything. Wisdom says I am
nothing. Between the two, my life flows.
—Nisargadatta Maharaj

I f you and I want to have peace and freedom, we must change the way
we live our lives. We must honor our authentic self, follow our Soul's
desires, and strengthen our self-will. The first steps are accepting who you
are and presenting your true self to the world.

Our early identity is formed from the interactions with people around
us and our environment. We interpret who we are by what people tell us
and how people make us feel. We also use cognitive thinking to understand and decipher the external world. As we develop and mature, our
partially formed ego and mindset discover a bigger world and we become
curious about our role in it. We learn to identify our value by what we do
and the success it brings. We depend on external markers to recognize

our worth. But there is a deeper, more complete identity that goes beyond the ego. If you feel your career is unsatisfying or you don't like how you present yourself to others, it is likely your current identity doesn't align with your Soul identity. You may be living within limits you learned rather than what your Soul demands.

Children experience a wide range of feelings as they grow and develop. There is a normal desire to express or display these new emotions. Reactions from others can make them feel ashamed of their true feelings, so children learn to hide their emotions from others and themselves. If a child screams in delight, for example, a parent may scold the child, teaching them that sheer bliss is negative. If you're not encouraged and praised as a child, you may learn that nothing you do is worthy. In cases when the spirit is severely wounded, children may inflict self-harm to punish themselves or control their negative feelings caused by others. The level of worthlessness is determined by what we perceive as our level of weakness. The more "bad" feelings or negative personality traits we have, the weaker we are. A strong chain has no weak links and we feel like the weak link. Worthlessness or self-criticism begin to dominate our lives. That's when we feel like a failure.

> It is the false shame of fools to try to conceal wounds that have not healed.
> —Horace

The Solar Plexus Chakra

The 3rd Chakra or energy center is called the Solar Plexus. The energy wheel is located just below your ribs at the top of your belly. It governs how you self-identify as well as how you express yourself. It is the seat of your core personality, your willpower, determination, self-control, self-esteem, and self-discipline. It contains the perception of who you are. If you are struggling to find your life purpose, it is likely that an imbalance in this energy system is at play. Healing makes it possible for your Soul's purpose and authentic self to emerge.

We are gifted with certain talents and capabilities for a purpose. You become fully actualized when you use your gifts. Negative emotions and negative habits can block this energy from functioning at its highest potential, thus keeping us just off-center enough to feel limited in life. Shame is a common emotion that can spin us out of control and it is the main emotion that creates imbalances in the 3rd, or Solar Plexus Chakra.

Jesse was a handsome boy, sensitive, aware, and always wanting to please. With a big heart and bigger dreams, he loved to perform and entertain others. He had a good relationship with his siblings and friends, but his parents were alcoholics. There was regular discord in the home that often escalated to yelling. Conflict and rage were common. Manipulation and shame were equally familiar to Jesse during his youth.

Jesse wasn't allowed to have feelings like normal kids. He was scolded or talked down to when he was excited or laughed too much. Although he was handsome, popular, and accomplished in school, his foundation of worthiness was not supported at home. He received little encouragement to develop his talents. His parents, caught in the web of addiction, did well to take care of themselves. The child's emotional welfare suffered as a result.

Jesse started to over-control his behavior in order to function. As a teenager, he stacked his shoes in perfect fashion. He detailed his car with immaculate precision and his wardrobe was spotless. When his orderly life was challenged, he responded with anger. Then he found his new lease on life. Hair.

In 1973, hair had a lot of power. Jesse learned that long and sexy hair was the recipe for attention. He discovered that people were fawning over men with wavy, long, and thick hair. He started using his hair to seek approval from women, his friends, and later from prospective employers. The hair became an obsession.

It wasn't until his early 20s that the self-destructive behavior developed. By this time an obsessive-compulsive disorder emerged. He spent countless hours styling and blow-drying his hair. A bad hair day would cause him to throw things at the mirror, beat his head with the brush, and send him back to the shower to start the process all over again. He couldn't leave the house without having every hair in place.

Multiple brushes, hairdryers, and pomade were necessary to achieve his desired result: the need for good hair and for acceptance. To him, perfect hair meant he was worthy of attention and love. At some point Jesse could no longer tolerate his feelings of unworthiness. He needed the hair to override his other feelings of shame. Jesse lived in a private hell.

Sadly, Jesse wasn't getting the results he wanted. There were no more girlfriends or acting jobs and no reward for his torture. The self-punishment became exhausting to his spirit. He started drifting into a psychological demise, losing control over his ability to go to work, to go to an audition, or feel accomplished in any way. Anger prompted him to seek help.

Shame

Children are like sponges. They absorb everything during their developmental years. Their heightened senses allow for a great deal of learning to take place. They are discovering who they are, their likes, and their dislikes. Unfortunately, they also absorb and believe what they hear and see, with little ability to discern the truth. Self-image and self-worth are established during these younger years. It's during this time that the child develops their sense of shame.

Shame is not just the feeling of doing wrong, it is the feeling of being wrong. There is a core belief behind shame that something is wrong with you. Shame makes you feel like you are not seen, loved, valued, or understood. It says you aren't good enough. It makes us feel improper, disgraceful, and dishonorable. Shame forces us to define ourselves by our weaknesses.

Shame is the natural result of the imperfections of human nature. It is part of our growth and each one of us may deal with it differently. Family members and others in the inner circle of a child's life will often make comments or judgments about the child's personality or behavior. Remarks such as "She's selfish" or "He's stubborn" leave a lasting impression on the child

> Shame is the most powerful master emotion. It's the fear that we're not good enough.
> —Brene Brown

and can become the foundation of shame. A parent may repeatedly infer a characteristic of shame by directing the child or person to *not* be something. "Don't be crazy" and "Don't be so sensitive" are common reprimands. The underlying message is that the child has a propensity to indeed be crazy or overly sensitive, and therefore something is wrong with them. Children internalize what they hear and this creates a framework of shame.

To help you better understand the grip that shame has on your life, think of three things that made you feel ashamed or embarrassed growing up. For example, it may be shame of sexuality, shame of being too pretty, or shame of being imperfect. In your journal, write and reflect on these feelings of shame.

In addition to shame, there are many triggers that can throw us into emotional distress. Long-standing issues may create problems later in our lives when they show up as negative patterns or behavioral disorders. The following is a list of possible emotional symptoms of an imbalanced Solar Plexus Chakra. Mark the ones that resonate with you.

Control issues   Cynicism

Emotional outbursts   Desire of power

Inability to take action   Selfishness

Lack of confidence   Neurosis

Self-harm   Need to dominate

Passivity   Worthlessness

Stubbornness   Fear of death

Aggression   Eating disorders

Self-criticism   Shaming others

Sarcasm   Lack of ambition

Lack of self-control   Type-A personality

Addiction   Loneliness

Competitiveness   Shaming Self

Sarcasm   Helplessness

OCD   Entitlement issues

Physical symptoms are also indicators that an energetic or emotional imbalance is at play. Chronic energy imbalances will eventually manifest in the body. Shame typically shows up early in our lives, which gives the shame a good deal of time to manifest itself as health issues in the body or mind. Some issues can be corrected or restored with persistent healing work, but in no way should you risk your health. Many imbalances can be adjusted with intention to better health, lower stress, and process emotions. Seek the advice of your physician to treat serious physical symptoms or ailments. The following are some physical symptoms of an imbalanced Solar Plexus.

Ulcers   Liver or gallbladder issues

Diabetes   Low stamina

Hypoglycemia   Digestive disorders

Fibromyalgia   Gas or bloating

Whereas women often carry excess and unprocessed energy in their 2nd or Sacral Chakra (the Feeling Center), men often store unprocessed emotions in this Solar Plexus energy center. Shame, coupled with the pressure that men feel to hide their emotions, often leads to an imbalance. As the Solar Plexus also governs our self-will, self-control, and aspects of our ego, it is not uncommon for people to have an over-abundance of energy in the Solar Plexus. Unexercised will-power, egotism, gluttony, and controlling behaviors often show up in an expansion of the belly region.

Shame is healed through sharing. Friends, family members, or support groups are worthwhile outlets to openly express who you are and how you feel. Find people who are compassionate listeners and talk about what you felt ashamed of growing up. Be honest and real and as transparent as possible. Sharing will start the restoration of your authentic self and is a healing antidote to shame. It's not about getting rid of or letting go of emotions, it's about fortifying your life with positive energy and people who will allow your shame to be free.

> Others' feelings toward you have nothing to do with your self-worth.

For Jesse, seeing a psychotherapist was somewhat therapeutic, but it didn't provide complete resolution to his problems. Jesse recalled the AA meetings his father went to for alcoholism, and he attended a similar type of support group. As he found connection to others through their stories and feelings, he found connection to himself. As the group shared feelings of self-doubts, shame, and self-loathing, the honesty that was shared nurtured his own truth to come forward. After almost four years of attending daily meetings, Jesse gained enough strength to confront his authentic feelings. His healing process began. His heart opened, his confidence soared, and his art flourished. He learned that connecting to his truth and expressing it to others were crucial to improving his health. Past efforts to control other people's responses to him proved fruitless.

As we become more mature in emotional healing, we can release the need to justify our experiences and our feelings. Sharing should be done openly with no explanations or qualifications needed.

> Shame is a soul-
> eating emotion.
> —C.G. Jung

I'll never forget driving down the highway from Reno, Nevada, to Tahoe City, California. It was a cold winter night and I was tired after a long day of college classes. For a period of time I lived in Tahoe and went to school in Reno, making the hour commute two days a week.

It was stressful to be away from my family and live in such a cold climate, but I loved being on my own, exploring the country and growing up as a young 20-something. This night was memorable because I was filled with remorse. The night before I fell back into the pit of my shame and binged on a gallon of ice cream.

It all started when I pulled into a convenience store and purchased a gallon of mint chocolate chip, my favorite flavor. I then drove around the lake, scooping it out with my fingers and shoving it in my mouth. The whole gallon. I thought I was done with this part of my life; it had been at least a year since my last purging episode. But stress had stacked up and my emotional foundation was weak. I was feeling anxious, afraid, and alone. I felt like the decisions I was making weren't right for me. I felt pressure to finish school. I missed my friends and family. And I dealt with it by swallowing my emotions.

I drove in circles while I ate. Like a dog trying to hide its bone, I looked for a place to hide my shame. I found a dark and private spot where I could purge the cold liquid that made my throat burn and my spirit weep. Within minutes out came the ice cream. On street corners, behind dumpsters, outside my car in a dark parking lot. The food that came up replaced the tears and emotions I wanted to release, but I didn't know how to do that in a way that felt safe. So, I binged and purged.

I recognized that familiar, lost place in my Soul. Since childhood, I felt like I didn't fit in even though I was popular at school. I didn't feel "heard" at home and felt insecure about my talents or dreams. I was always too this or too that. Instead of turning for help, I turned to food. I used food as a tool to control my negative emotions. Food offered both self-comfort and self-torture during my high school years and I relied on both to satisfy my shame. When I developed warning signs in my chest and stomach, I soon became scared I was going to cause permanent damage to myself. I knew I needed help.

I was desperate to do something different. As I drove home from school that next night from Reno, I had to make a choice about how I would handle my emotional hell. Binging and purging no longer seemed an option. My shame was deeper than before. I needed something, a quick fix. So, I pulled into a convenient store and bought cigarettes.

When I was a kid I hated when my dad smoked. I would cry and ask him to stop hurting himself. Later, I remembered the disgust I felt when my classmates smoked in our first years of college and I had turned my nose up at them. I flashed back through those memories, but at this juncture of my life I was desperate for something to help me stop the binge and purge cycle. Smoking seemed a better option than throwing up. From that day forward I never binged and purged again. For the next several years I smoked just enough every day to control my emotional appetite.

It's not uncommon to replace one negative behavior for another. We do this to try to affect change in our lives without disturbing our emotional pitfalls. It's a game we play, like a personal fake-out.

Bulimia, like many other negative behaviors, is a form of control. When a person is desperately afraid of their authentic (and often negative) feelings, they create new destructive patterns of self-torture or other pain. It's easier to control one's own response to self-imposed shame rather than the shame others may inflict. We believe that the shame others inflict must be true and often that feels unmanageable. We tell ourselves that we cannot change something that is true, so the new, self-imposed shame becomes the focal point. It allows us to keep buried our personal wounded feelings deep within. Eating disorders in general, as well as other coping mechanisms, feed the void of the emotional pit. It is often the case that one is not getting the emotional nurturing one needs, or is unable to process the emotional distress, so they attempt to control their own sustenance by controlling food. There are many variables and theories available on the subject, but in general eating disorders are tangible ways to express the emptiness we feel inside. It is displayed by lack of sustenance or by abuse of sustenance.

Feeling an empty void is common for many people. The black pit or dissatisfaction is a result of disconnection from our Source and our Soul. There is nothing great enough to fill the internal void of worthlessness, self-doubt, or shame except strength that comes from connectivity to all that is. This is the power of Oneness, of connection. The more we access this eternal Source, the more confident and "full" we fill in life.

It's not possible to reach your full potential if you're emotionally detached. Like physical massage for the body, emotional healing provides new circulation and regeneration by getting into the tight or restricted feelings. By breaking up the hardened tissues, new life is generated in the body, allowing blood and oxygen to flow freely. Pain is then reduced.

Emotional healing is paramount to achieve true purpose and happiness. With balanced and healthy energy patterns, you are better prepared to take action and meet challenges in your life. To fully realize your greatest potential and purpose, you should function in healthy ways in all elements of yourself, including your emotions. Being at your best requires stamina, will-power, and the desire and dedication to get up each morning and fulfill your life's work. Remaining stuck in emotional pain is not in your best interest. Just as you can't achieve great physical feats without exercise and commitment to health, the same is true for emotional health. You need to be at your best to perform at your best. Excelling in life requires you to bring your emotional a-game.

All life purposes are created equal. Your purpose may be to care for one individual in a nursing home or to be the mother of the next Thomas Edison. Your purpose may be to invent a device that will save lives. To live your Soul's desire is one of the deepest expressions of self-love. To fulfill your dreams and be the best that you can be requires harnessing the energy of your will and living from your core essence, your authentic self. Some people have dreams of simple survival; others dream of receiving the Nobel Peace Prize. Both serve humanity equally. Your talents and gifts are never frivolous.

> There is no other greater ecstasy than to know who you are.
> —Osho

One of the many traps of shame is to make us believe we are something we are not. If we believe in our shame, we identify with our weakness. I often hear people defend their poor behavior with words such as "But that's just who I am!" That is not "who they are" at all. That is just a representation of their negative self-identity shrouded in shame. Although some people claim they want relief from their suffering and would like a better life, they don't know how to get free of their shame. They get trapped in their negative patterns until they believe they are "impatient" or "unworthy" or "insensitive."

Laziness is a factor, as emotional processing can be work, but much of our negative patterning corresponds to the habits and routines we set in accordance with what we believe to be our weakest link. Then we claim that for ourselves. Who you are is not limited by any of the negative habits or characteristics that you have displayed or that others say about you.

Who you are is love and light; you are pure in nature and capable of growth and evolution. If you apply yourself, you can meet the nature of your Soul.

Emotional Workout

Child-Like Heart: On a piece of paper, list three things you loved to do as a child, such as color, build forts, bake cookies, and so forth. I loved to dance and run around with a microphone interviewing family members. Underneath, list three things you love to do as an adult—things you feel skilled at or just enjoy doing. Is there any overlap? At the bottom of the page, write a word or job description that combines at least one of the activities from both lists.

Your authenticity is born in the Soul. Your Soul begs for an expression of your genuine and unique voice as it searches for a place in your everyday existence. When you accept its request, your life takes on a more substantial meaning. But first you must wade through the false truths of your identity that was learned earlier in life. You must reclaim the person you truly are and heal the parts of your identity that others have tainted. Only then can you trust the expression of your authentic purpose.

Sandy came to me out of desperation. She was an attorney but had not practiced in a year due to alcoholism. On the outside, she seemed to have it all. She was smart and beautiful with a healthy family and supportive environment. On the inside, she was shrouded in suffering from fear and shame. She hid her shame by escaping into the world of alcohol. Confronting the world, face to face, was a challenge to her.

She told me she was afraid. I asked her to identify the fear so she could see that she was hiding from herself, not something in the world. She replied, "I have no idea; there's nothing that can be that scary. It just feels like it will be." That was shame speaking.

Sandy was almost too smart for her own good. You may know people like her. They can talk themselves into or out of any situation, rationalizing, over-analyzing, worrying, and controlling with their mind. Even though she could discuss her issues with others, she couldn't allow herself to connect with her body and her feelings. She was blocking her shame. Sadly, her family was over-protective and tried to shield her from facing her feelings, which made her situation worse.

She made tremendous strides as we worked together. Sandy took classes to reinstate her license and made plans for her future, and she regularly attended meditation class. But Sandy continued to struggle with her true emotions and the pain of her shame. Eventually, she went to group rehab, where she was removed from all stimuli and enabling patterns. In that closed environment without support of the bottle and her family and friends, she broke down the walls to her shame.

> Thinking will not overcome fear, but action will.
> —W. Clement Stone

Many people struggle to identify the fear or emotion that creates the block. The more they disengage with self, becoming lost in the distractions of the external world, it becomes hard to decipher the internal world. Returning to harbored emotions such as shame can be overwhelming. But our bodies will tolerate only so much avoidance before serious health implications arise.

Love will heal your shame. Acceptance of your authentic self is the link to your healing. As you accept your true feelings, your self-love deepens. Through the lens of love your life becomes meaningful. You are meant to be here on Earth. You have unique talents, gifts, and a purpose that the world needs to maintain homeostasis. No matter what you may have believed in the past, you have a unique reason for being and your presence matters immensely. You are the only one who can fulfill your specific purpose but you must be proactive in matters of the heart, mind, and emotion. Life is challenging and not easy to navigate, but the climb to the mountaintop is worth the investment to witness the incredible views.

Emotional Workout

Energy Medicine: In working with shame, energy healing can provide a nice and subtle beginning to shift the difficult feelings of insecurity, self-criticism, and worthlessness. Find a compassionate practitioner in the healing arts such as Polarity Therapy, Healing Touch, or other hands-on healing. Find a healing circle where you can experience various practitioners. There are many energy healing modalities that utilize movement and the breath that are extremely powerful, such as Yoga, Qigong, Tai Chi, and others. Explore. Find the right environment that allows you to feel safe to move and connect mind and breath to body. Most of all, find a place where you can be yourself.

Healthy Shame

Shame can serve us in positive ways. Healthy shame is a barometer of our morals and our value system. If we have harmed or wronged someone, shame alerts us that we have gone against our own principles, which makes us feel poorly. Healthy shame encourages us to make amends and repair the damage that we've caused. When we employ healthy shame, the rectification of a situation makes us feel good again.

Achieving a balanced emotional life requires the use of healthy shame. When the two kinds of shame get intermingled, behaviors such as entitlement, selfishness, humiliation, criticism of others, sarcasm, and shaming others become normal and toxic responses. If we do not take responsibility for our actions and thoughts that hurt others, we inflict more shame on ourselves. Apologizing for our misuse of shame on others is a positive form of self-care.

Emotional Workout

Rectification: Making amends for our actions can be difficult. To restore balance and integrity to our authentic self, begin the practice of rectification now. Name two people whom you have hurt by action or words. Write a sincere apology to one of these people. They may never read it, but pretend as if they will. Write with compassion.

Is your spirit nudging and alerting you that something is missing? Are you seeking a deeper sense of gratification and peace? It's not always the work that defines your gratification, but it is certainly the attitude and energy you bring to your work. If you are present with your Soul's purpose, it doesn't matter about the actual job. Like the adage, it's not what you do, it's how you do it.

Nisargadatta Maharaj was an Indian guru. He has written many texts and books on mindfulness, self-awareness, and enlightenment. His teachings have helped thousands of people from all backgrounds of life. He is one of the wisest teachers and thinkers of all time, yet he made his living rolling cigarettes in a shop he owned in India. In the need to provide for self, one does what one needs to do, and that's what he did. He wasn't upset by it or afraid of losing his identity, nor was he affected by the triviality of his job. Instead, he harnessed the power of his Soul work to become a tremendous asset to humanity at large.

Living an authentic life is the realization that what you do matters less than who you are. It's the expression of your Soul's longing that is important, and that affirmation can come alive behind the counter at a retail store, in a corporate office, or at home caring for children.

Your life purpose may not seem grandiose, but if you recognize that all life is connected, each menial job is just as important as any other. You may not be the one who invented the computer, but you may be the person who helps build the machines in the factory. Without the working computer available for use, the invention would have little value.

Don't ever believe that your contribution isn't as important or impactful as the greatest job in the world. The important thing is to live your authentic purpose in some regard, whether in your work or in your daily life. Every job is important and each role makes the world a better place.

> We do not have to be ashamed of what we are. As sentient beings we have wonderful backgrounds. The backgrounds may not be particularly enlightened or peaceful or intelligent. Nevertheless, we have soil good enough to cultivate; we can plant anything in it.
> —Chogyam Trungpa

The amount of money you make does not identify who you are or what your Soul wants in life. A person's life purpose is not defined by making money. Some want to believe it is, but that's an empty quest of an imbalanced ego. The ego finds great reward and often identifies success in the world in this way. There's nothing wrong with making a good living. It feels rewarding and allows you to help others with resources or investments in the progress of education, health, or the arts. Greed and money, however, can easily create imbalances in our authentic happiness.

How do you define yourself? Not by what you do, but how you identify yourself. List three descriptions that identify you and your purpose. Start your sentence with "I am. . . ."

The Grass Is Always Greener

"The grass is always greener" mentality has the potential to create more shame and separation. The greener grass theory means that "over there" is better than "right here." It means who you are or what you've experienced isn't enough. The media has helped exacerbate this problem. "Over there" is better, prettier, more successful. When you get "there" you won't suffer. "There" may be after your divorce. After you lose 20 pounds. After you get the promotion. When you make more money.

This mentality is a fantasy, providing no hope for healing or happiness in the present. In hoping that life is better "over there" than your current reality, you become lazy in your creativity. You parlay responsibilities to family, work, or community. You don't deal with your real emotions. You put off the possibility of peace and joy to another time, believing that the environment will affect change in your inner world. You wait for happiness after work. After a glass of wine. After a nap. This mindset masks the true emotion of the moment. It is the opposite of mindfulness. "There is better than here" sets us up for constant disappointment. It's a form of self-sabotage. In emotional healing there is no here or there, only now or later. To realize that "later" is simply "now" at a different point in time is a door to awakening. To be conscious and connected to our authentic self we choose now.

I've found that sometimes we need to be in the wrong place to get the motivation we need to get to the right place. When I first moved to New York City I worked at a temp agency. The job paid the bills but I was bored out of my mind. Every day felt like a drain. This was not the reason I moved to Manhattan. I was drifting down the wrong creek. As days turned into months, my angst increased. My Soul was grinding against a concrete wall. I tinkered away the days filing papers as my spirit grew numb. My dream was to create wellness media in the Big Apple, but out of fear, I was settling for less. Each day grew longer and my Soul became impatient. The more I tried to settle the storm brewing inside, the more flustered I became. One day I couldn't ignore my Soul any longer. I had to get back on my path or I was going to explode. So, I quit my job and refocused my energies. I was not lead astray.

Have you ever felt this way? It's called friction. And it's not a bad thing if you learn to utilize it. Friction can set your pants on fire and get you moving toward change. Like pulling a slingshot back, the resistance gets just so tight that it will break unless you release the grip and let it soar.

What Do You Hide Behind?

It's not unusual to conceal low self-worth or shameful feelings. People hide behind their jobs or other activities to avoid listening and developing the skills needed to fulfill their Souls. The list of things we hide behind is long with behaviors like fear, excessive shopping, denying enjoyment, using false identities, and over-eating. The protective layer of fat can be a safe hiding place for emotional strife. The excess tissue is used to store our negative feelings and block access to intimacy or self-discovery. Some people try to hide behind a pretense of spirituality or some type of diet. If they hide well enough, they think their shameful truth is camouflaged. But they are not peaceful warriors with open hearts or calm minds. They are riddled with self-doubt, anxiety, perfectionism, worthlessness, grief, and other attributes accumulated over the harrowing years. I've hidden behind bulimia. I've hidden behind vegetarianism or other controlled measures. We replace one action for another to counter our shame, fear, guilt, and negative feelings. We lose the opportunity to strengthen these positive aspects of our being when we hide behind these scapegoats.

Our sense of self is fortified when we use our gifts and talents. Spirits ignite as we feel in tune with our Souls. Just like a muscle needing to be exercised, your sense of self-worth and all the attributes that make you strong must be used as well. Will-power, determination, self-confidence, self-control, and healthy boundaries all need regular exercise. There's always potential in the muscle, but it requires regular use. As a practicing massage therapist, I saw the pain that weak muscles can cause. Many people believe soreness comes from tightness, but it can also be caused by underused, weak muscles. Muscles are meant to do a job and work. A healthy muscle doesn't react with pain; it just performs its job. There's a good feeling from proper exercise and a healthy body. There's a cleansing feeling from a good cry. There's great nourishment in hearty laughter. The more we work out our emotions, the stronger and healthier we will become.

Emotional Workout

Project Planning: Everyone has a dream. It could be a business venture or creative in nature. Maybe it's sailing around the world or a song to be composed. Making horizontal lines, divide a piece of paper in three sections. Title the first section your "Project." Under the title, write a paragraph that describes the goal you want to accomplish and why. It may seem silly, but press forward. Name the second section "Outline." In this section you will make a list of the items you need, the tasks to accomplish, and the materials and resources necessary to complete your project. Don't become overwhelmed or sidetracked regarding costs. Just write down what is needed to reach your dream goal. The third section will be titled "Time line." Create a reasonable estimation, from start to finish, of when you will complete your task. Whether you act on it or not is at your discretion, but at a minimum finish this exercise. At the end of the third section, put a target date of completion. Review your work. If you would like to move forward with you goal, draw two lines at the bottom of the page. Sign one and date the other. This is your contract.

Action

Many people seek reactions from people. These are vain attempts to get attention or control a situation. Reactions feed egos, responses cultivate relationships. A reaction puts the other person in control. A response is a thoughtful action that allows equal participation in the conversation or activity. Positive actions and responses allow you to have healthy engagement with the world around you.

If you are not strong in action, you are weak in reactions. There's a great difference between the positive energy of action and the negative energy of reaction. One is protective and powerful, the other is defensive and weak.

Protection

Are people in your life draining your energy? We often refer to these people as "energy vampires." Like masses of toxic goo, they feel heavy and burdensome to be around. They emit a negative vibe and seem to threaten our space. The truth is that no one can drain your energy or become an energy vampire if you don't allow them to control your response to their actions or energies. We give so much power to other people and energies that we are scared—and often on the defensive.

> Do not learn how to react, learn how to respond.
> —Buddha

People often ask me, "How do I protect myself from negative, toxic people?" The answer is to get in the power position. Become a strong and solid energy with a confident presence and stop defending yourself against others. The defense position means you crouch in the corner and put up your arms while the offense comes charging at you. I always think of a boxing match. In any moment, there's the fighter who is swinging, and the opponent who is defending the swing. This is similar to the way many people live. They are scared and spend their time blocking or running from negative blows. Without becoming aggressive or offensive, imagine standing tall and confident with your strong pillar of emotional strength and energy beaming from every orifice of your body. If anyone swings at that, it would be like swinging at a brick wall. Negativity can't compete with the powerful positive vibrations you emit.

You lose your power when you believe others have the ability to sway your peace. The same is true for energetic protection of all kinds. Even though Modern Sage sells crystals and sage that are believed to be powerful protection items, the best protection you can have is to strengthen your core. Stay connected to who you are and every experience that has built you. Strengthen your resolve to live, to be free, to be whole. This happens as you heal. As you awaken to self-love.

Depletion (exhaustion) is counter to what you may think. It isn't caused from doing too much. It's caused from doing too little of the right thing. When you apply life-force energy on things that matter, you will not feel depleted. You will feel energized. Feeling like you don't have more to give means your own resources are spinning out of control. It's a sign that you are misfiring, misgiving, or need a tune-up. Your vibration is less than your Soul's target.

> Do not spend your precious energy protecting yourself from negative vibrations of others. Strengthen your own, becoming a force of power—impenetrable.

Projecting or asserting our beliefs on others is a drain on our energy. My mother once taught me a lesson about caring for plants. A dying leaf will continue to pull energy from nutrients that the rest of the plant needs. If you cut back the part that is lifeless, the rest of the plant will become stronger with more energy. Giving your energy to a person who is not asking for it or is not responsive to your help saps your own nutrients. If you go too far with this, you risk becoming an emotional martyr, using someone else as an excuse for your personal neglect and negative feelings.

Don't worry about what the other person is doing. Focus on yourself. What can you do to become stronger? If you find yourself focused or fixated on a particular person or situation, it may be a sign you need to create a safer and stronger core pillar. If your core pillar is not strong, you will leak vital energy and allow unwanted negativity to come in from others. I think of it like holes in the body. Where we are weak and underdeveloped emotionally, we become susceptible to the penetration of negativity. We should fill those weak holes with fortitude, confidence, and will. Use the Emotional Workouts and processes to strengthen your foundation and self-identity.

Emotional Workout

Boundaries: Use this breathing meditation to strengthen your personal boundaries. Energy is real and it is powerful. Learn to expand your energy and become strong. Close your eyes and take a deep inhale. Allow a natural exhale. Do not force it. Imagine there is an invisible bubble around your entire body. It may look like a thin soap bubble. With each inhale, imagine that the bubble gently expands in all directions. Breathe slow and with great intention, as you don't want your bubble to burst! As you exhale and the bubble stays in place, imagine that your bubble continues to strengthen and expand with your breath. This thin film surrounding you is your aura. As you breathe and focus, you are increasing your energy.

Control

Helping others to find better ways to live their lives can actually be a form of control on our part. Although our hearts are convinced we just want to "help," there is a healthy way to help people that doesn't drain you nor does it take control away from the other person.

Help and control are very different actions. The person we are helping must be willing to receive assistance. If they are unwilling, you are placed in the control position. Some of us like to be in control. It makes us feel powerful and worthy, and we willingly assert our beliefs for others to follow. But in the balance of emotional healing, particularly regarding healing shame, we must be careful not to issue commands. Control can be dangerous in three ways:

1. Controlling others against their will.
2. Over-controlling our own lives.
3. Having no self-control.

If you help a person who is seeking assistance, your help feels like love. There may be some tough love involved, but both parties are engaged and willing. Regardless of the outcome, loving help is usually welcomed and feels like a positive effort. Controlling someone against their will is not positive unless there is danger involved. For example, controlling a person's choice of career is selfish and based in fear or greed. Not allowing your spouse to weigh in on how the family budget is spent is manipulation. Making degrading comments about an adult's choice of style is based on your own insecurity. These types of control are negative and reveal your personal shame or insecurities.

Over-controlling our personal lives is an attempt to hide behind our shame and anxieties. As mentioned previously, people control their shame in a multitude of ways: rebelling against parents, limiting or obsessing over diet and foods, performing various types of self-torture, creating fears or phobias, being overly rigid, OCD, and anal retentive behavior to name a few.

The other extreme is a lack of self-control. A determination to lose weight is easily swayed by one Little Debbie. A resolve to end the affair is trumped by loneliness. A lack of self-control stems from the weakness of your shame. It confirms that we have little trust in our self-worth; instead we fall back into our weakness.

Having healthy control is essential. Someone should be in control over most any situation. Be it God, you, or the pilot. For the things we cannot control, learning to trust is necessary. Trust of this nature becomes easier as we trust more in ourselves. If you have confidence in yourself, in your beliefs, and your abilities, trusting others becomes more natural.

Trust in self can be improved by opening your heart. As you open your heart, you will engage more fully in activities and you will have greater desire to perform at your peak level. As you engage and give life your best, you begin to see positive results and may receive possible compliments, which reinforce positive behavior and self-worth. Your reality shifts and it's more likely that you will believe other people are engaged and caring in their work as well.

Emotional Workout

Core Training: To strengthen your emotional and energetic core, start by strengthening your physical core. I recommend sit-ups and backbends. Include 10 to 25 sit-ups or crunches into your weekly exercise routine three to four times a week to strengthen and tighten the core muscles in your stomach. Also, include some type of back-bend. If you are stiff or inflexible, start by lying on your back with bent knees. Place your feet on the floor near your bottom. Lift your hips to the sky and keep your arms and hands on the floor. Breathe into your belly. With these exercises, you lengthen, as well as contract, the core muscles in your body.

Not everyone will gain your trust, but with a new internal confidence, you can put down the reigns and allow the other person to do their job. That goes for God or the airline pilot. Having healthy self-control and self-image strengthens your trust in others. As you begin to genuinely trust your actions, you can trust life experiences.

The Power of Your Will

Denying your feelings is one of the quickest ways to weaken your will. Your will is directly connected to your core purpose and Soul. When you trap emotions within, you suffocate or dampen your will. The nature of your will is to be free. Anything less is detrimental. Your will needs the freedom to choose. Part of your will's job is to accept reality and move through it anyway. It is truth that allows the will to flourish, even if the truth is difficult to accept.

When you allow your will to express itself, you live in harmony with your Soul. Your presence is powerful and noticeable; you become the example of strength and health. Living in accordance with your authentic self means you accept who you truly are. You live the expression of that truth and become a source of inspiration for others.

It is not your nature to shrink or be weak in thought, emotion, or will. Nature does not generally rebirth into weaker form. That is not a sign of good health. If you live from an undetermined will, you will remain weak. Positive change and spiritual evolution is not possible from a weakened state of being.

The nature of life is to expand and to grow. As we evolve as a species, as energy, as thought, we do not become more fragile, we become stronger and more intelligent. Evolution requires that weaker aspects of life fall away and transform.

Employ your will. Do more of what your gut tells you and proclaim who you are. Challenge yourself to finish. People fill the hours of the day on menial tasks or taking care of the needs of others. Become a do-er of your purpose. Take time to follow-through with the needs of your Self. This is not about fitting in a jog or a trip to the nail salon. It includes real self-care. Rest your Soul, listen to your higher power, or be of service in a way that is meaningful to you.

If you are running from your purpose or distracting yourself from your calling, you are sabotaging and draining vital life-force energy that is meant to be in action. Muscles are meant to work. Emotions are meant to process. Your purpose should be put to use.

Solar Plexus Chakra Basics

Color: Yellow

Gemstones: Citrine, Tiger's Eye, Topaz, Malachite, Calcite

Essential Oils: Cinnamon, Juniper Berry, Lavender, Geranium, Ginger, Vetiver, Grapefruit, Black Pepper, Chamomile, Fennel, Neroli

Meditation

Start by focusing on your breath. Allow the breath to flow freely in and out. After a few breaths, close your eyes and imagine you are walking barefoot on the soft, cool earth. Each inhale and exhale equals one step forward. After several breaths, you approach a small mud hut in the shape of an igloo. Inhale as you pull the door open; exhale as you crouch down to step through the curved doorway. Take yourself to the center of this domed structure, and as you exhale, sit gently on the ground. Feel the cool earth beneath you and the smell of minerals and water in the air. Inhale. As you exhale, the door quietly shuts, leaving the hut almost entirely dark. There's no fear; you feel safe and protected, as if in the womb. Close your eyes and just breathe. As you inhale use the mantra "I am" and on the exhale, just listen. Again, inhale "I am." Exhale, listen. As you listen you may hear the words of your inner truth. Use those words on the exhale. "I am a teacher" or "I am worthy" or "I am an artist." Whatever positive aspiration you hear in the confines of this nurturing and safe hut, repeat it to yourself with this mantra. You may hear many empowering words. "I am." "I am." Spend time breathing and listening. When you are ready, mindfully exit the small hut and walk back to the present moment.

PART II
Awaken

CHAPTER 4

Oasis

Life begins where fear ends.

—Osho

It's time to get real and shine a big, bright light on what is going on in our inner worlds. There is pain and sorrow in many of our hearts that keeps us living at the emotional poverty line. Fear is the main reason we accept this state of being. We fear our feelings, failure, and even success. Primarily, we fear the pain that love can bring. You may think, "If I love, I will hurt," or "Love, like all other things, will end." To avoid the depth of pain, we avoid the depth of love. We know the desire and the energy it takes to make changes in our lives. We also know how fear can

> The root of all fear is disconnection.
>
>

grip us and affect our choices. The only way to heal the heart is to change your perspective of fear.

The root of all fear is disconnection, and it is this fear that keeps the door to our hearts, and love, closed. The ultimate disconnection from the self is death. Self-imposed suffering results when we try to stop change in our lives. The fear that "something" will become "nothing" (death) keeps us stuck in a negative emotional pattern. You may not fear physical death, but death can be feared in other ways. Think about the fear of change, for example. Change is perceived as the end of what we've known and leads us to the great void of the unknown.

Thankfully, the Soul never dies. People, places, and things may change, but the energy of the Soul remains constant. We do not die, we simply transform. The appropriate response to our emotions or our hopes is not to "Let It Go" but to "Let It Change." If you allow change, there will be no need to force any other response. What is meant to be at this time will be. To attempt to change that fact causes unnecessary grief. When something different is required, it will change. This is the nature of evolution. There is no death of energy or Soul. In fact, it is transformation that makes life possible.

Many people feel they have a dark cloud over them. They think they are "cursed" and they search for something to break them out of a "spell." It's as if something overhead is looming and they can't escape. What they feel is a dark cloud of pent-up emotional energy that is ready to release and transform.

> The purpose of a cloud is not to block your light, but to nourish your life.

In fifth grade I dreamed of becoming a meteorologist, mostly because I learned to say the word. It didn't work out, but my interest inspired me to learn more about clouds and water. The Earth is more than 70 percent water. Our bodies are about 60 percent water. Water is fluid. If our bodies are predominantly fluid and the Earth is predominantly fluid, can we not assume our state of being should be fluid as well? Our emotions are also fluid, like the changing tide.

Clouds are an important part of the water cycle. They hold and drop moisture from the sky, feeding the earth's eco systems. When the water on the earth evaporates, water is turned back to vapor. Plants use a process called transpiration, which is the evaporation of water from the tiny holes in the leaves, and transmits vapor back into the air. As the water in the air cools, it condenses and the condensation becomes clouds. The clouds become heavy and eventually some form of precipitation falls to the ground. A dark cloud is just thick, denser particles of held moisture— the thicker the cloud becomes, the less light can penetrate through it.

I'd like to tell you a story about a cloud named Calvin. Calvin loved being a cloud. One day Calvin received scary news from the other clouds. They said that soon he must release his moisture, which would totally change his look, shape, and his essence. He would never be the same cloud again. This terrified Calvin and he panicked. He collected and stored every drop of moisture that came his way. As Calvin's moisture started to increase, he became darker and heavier. He did not like what he was becoming. Calvin was convinced he would have to do something soon because he couldn't handle the pressure much longer.

Calvin managed to find a little courage so he dropped some moisture, then more and more. As Calvin's cloud continued to rain down, he noticed that his droplets were nourishing the soil and growing beautiful flowers. His precipitation was also watering the rivers and lakes, and people of all ages were dancing in the streets in the rain. Calvin loved his contribution to the world and, although he wasn't the same as before, he felt more alive than ever. He realized that change didn't mean death, but instead it offered a new form of life that was helping the natural processes of the world. Without his rain falling, the flowers and rivers and harvests would not be possible.

Our emotions, like water molecules, will eventually transform from our immediate physical and emotionally bodies. As each emotion "cools down" it condenses to form a "cloud" in our energy system. The cloud will release bits of precipitation as needed when another incident or memory calls for a particular emotion. If we stop the process of this natural cycle in our ecosystem, we will collect too many emotions in our cloud, which may feel heavy and scary. The weight then causes depression, emotional weakness, and the inability to move freely in our lives. Long term, unattended emotions may result in Post Traumatic Emotional Disorder (PTED).

PTED presents itself with symptoms such as insomnia, anxiety, tics and twitches, depression, avoidance behavior, addictions, or other maladies. The tendency is to treat the symptom instead of the unresolved emotions that created the symptom. To heal, you must find the courage to allow all emotions to be present in your life and to process them.

Have you ever been told that you will "get over it" or that you should "just get over it"? Although time helps mend the sharpness of our pain, it is how we address the emotion of a situation that determines our health and happiness. "Just get over it" is the street lingo for "Let It Go." You can't process or heal using this advice.

There is no pole-vaulting over reality. Allow yourself to stay in the process of healing and the reality of emotional energy. Every time I think of the rape or any other trauma, I experience an emotion. The feeling is always changing; that is the result of time and transformation. As the emotion shifts, it requires me to be malleable in heart and mind. Experiencing emotion doesn't mean I'm "not over it," it means that I'm in the process with it. My experience lives in me and is part of my pillar.

You may believe that if you don't have emotion about something or someone that you are "over it." Perhaps what you mean is that you aren't reacting to the trigger of the painful emotion in the present, which is positive. But the energy of emotion never dies, so it is impossible not to have some feeling about the matter. It's likely that you may be numb or denying the emotion. You are experiencing apathy. Everything causes a feeling and we should accept that. There's nothing more brave and courageous than honoring and accepting the truth of what is.

Like life, love transforms through suffering. The desire to heal begins in the heart. Self-care is critical to physical, emotional, and mental healing. We have the capacity to rejuvenate and recover from many of life's struggles. Just as the body has an intrinsic ability to heal itself, our emotional body uses our innate desire to survive to overcome the obstacles and challenges we face.

The Heart Chakra

The 4th, or Heart Chakra, is called the "Center of Love and Emotion" and is the "center-peace" of emotional healing. An open heart is like an internal oasis, a sanctuary to retreat to and find peace in our day-to-day living. This is where the passions of our Souls are translated into passions of our lives. It's a place of refuge and connection. If pain replaces love and openness the oasis becomes barren both figuratively and literally, and the heart clogs and hardens.

The denial or disconnection from our genuine emotions may make us ill, or at least emotionally blocked. When the flow of healthy energy throughout our body is stifled or out of balance, physical manifestations of blocked heart energy appear.

I've had people tell me I shouldn't get angry or experience negative emotions because I teach meditation or do healing work. It confirms a general belief that we should control and stifle our feelings for good mental and emotional health. But stifling feelings is the cause of emotional denial in the first place. It's not dangerous or "bad" to have emotions. The danger is in hiding, denying, or repressing emotions. This is where behaviors such as rage, self-harm, manipulation, and abuse generally develop. Expressing your feelings doesn't equate to intimidation, hurt, or blame, nor does it require violent acts. These responses to emotions may occur after years of *not* emoting in a healthy fashion. If you experience these emotional responses in your life, I encourage you to get in touch with your inner self and explore your feelings. Secondary emotional symptoms are the result of pain not being addressed. Do not negate the importance of how you feel or deny the presence of your emotions.

What emotion is real for you right now? Do you feel trapped? Is anger, resentment, or fear blocking your heart? These are genuine feelings that are too often disregarded in effort to act calm, controlled, or politically correct. We are not killing others with kindness, we are killing ourselves by not accepting the truth of what we feel. Physical symptoms of a blocked heart energy may include the following:

Angina	Asthma
Weakness	Lung disease
Heart palpitations	Shoulder problems
Heart attack	Poor circulation
Upper back issues	Respiratory conditions

More prevalent are the emotional and energetic manifestations of a blocked heart. Unprocessed emotions such as grief or sadness morph into other forms of distress including:

Anxiety	Depression
Isolation	Envy
Fatigue	Hopelessness
Inability to love	Despair
Apathy	Moodiness
Shyness	Jealousy
Loneliness	Inability to receive
Holding grudges	Social Anxiety

Think of the heart as a door hinge. Each side of the door is only accessible if the hinge operates properly. Otherwise, you can only enter or exit, or the door gets jammed altogether. The door to your heart allows your higher energy systems to communicate with your lower energy systems to accomplish healing. For example, if you have difficulty meditating and have a blocked 6th Chakra, you may need to work on grounding (1st Chakra) to stabilize your feelings of safety in higher spiritual energies. The heart is the bridge between the energy systems. An imbalance typically means more than one area needs attention. Your energy system is holistic and integrated, needing all areas to be available and responsive.

A person with an open heart exudes a sense of confidence. They have a greater sense of self-trust. Employing a wide range of authentic emotions is true self-love, and self-love comes from compassion. Compassion is care in action. It's more than feeling sorry for someone, or trying to understand the plight of another. It's giving attention and care toward genuine emotions. Be gentle with yourself while you grieve or treat yourself to other forms of self-care. Compassion can be acts of kindness such as listening, lending a hand, or donating to a family. Compassion comes from the vast and fluid space that is created from an open heart. From this oasis, you can allow, accept, and give.

Emotional Workout

Service to Others: Being of service to someone or something that needs your help is an option for you to rebalance your Heart Chakra energy. Seek people or causes that will allow and receive your attention. Get involved, even if it is only for an hour a week. Notice how empowering and good it feels to help another person, even if it is a stranger. Compensation is not important. It's about using your presence and skills for the good of humanity. This practice is a simple and effective approach to enhancing your personal power and strength.

Love

To know love is to know heartbreak. Love is the strongest of emotions yet it is the most fragile. Love is elusive yet it is the driving force of our lives. We chase it, run from it, abuse it, and block it. We manipulate others with the power of love. Love rules your perspective of life.

Regardless of our respective beliefs, it is generally agreed that sin translates as a fault, estrangement, or some type of violation. It may also be construed as negative actions or wrong-doing. It's a negative connotation that includes a wide range of shortcomings, including fear.

It's not uncommon for people to develop a phobia about their negative emotions and use almost any measure to block their feelings. We fear love; we fear to give or receive. We fear the pain of heartbreak because the more we love, the more potential we have for pain. As we shut down the capacity to give or receive love, we also shut down trust, passion, and the ability to create.

Jessica attended a session to work on fertility. She and her husband had tried to conceive but it wasn't happening. As I coached her through the first healing session, it became clear that she had energy blockages in her heart and sacral areas, along with a weak grounding presence. An art therapist, her career allowed her to creatively express herself as well as help others, but part of Jessica's core belief and emotional integrity wasn't connecting. Jessica had residual grief and a fear of motherhood. The grief from her childhood gripped her heart and kept her child-like heart closed. She'd forgotten how to love herself and enjoy life.

Due to grief, Jessica doubted her ability (and desire) to love and be a good

> Above all, love each other deeply, because love covers over a multitude of sins.
> —1 Peter 4:8,
> The Bible, New International Version

mother. The grief was latched to the fear of losing her self-identity and losing love again. We worked on opening the Sacral Energy Chakra (2nd), but Jessica also needed time to process the grief and work on self-love. She needed frivolous play time to let her inner child free. She also needed time alone to discern her true feelings about becoming a mother.

Jessica came back to see me several months later. She looked great. She was present, grounded, and centered. With a glimmer in her eye she told me about the summer nights she spent frolicking on the beach, nights out with her girlfriends, and romantic date nights with her husband. She was having the time of her life. She had processed what she learned about grief, the healing of her self-love, and the fear of loving again. Her heart felt light and free. And, at the time of her last visit, Jessica was two months pregnant!

This is not to say that energy healing and emotional coaching were entirely responsible for Jessica's pregnancy. But there is great power in the desire to heal, and in my work I've witnessed my clients achieve transformative life changes such as infertility to fertility, anxiety to joy, and grief to love. Jessica used her resolve to transform her life. She took her self-love work seriously and was able to unleash the stronghold that grief and the guilt of self-love had put on her. This power to heal is present in all of us.

Grief

Grief is heavy in the heart of human suffering. It serves as the main emotional block of the heart. Grief is a normal reaction to heartache and loss of any kind. Unprocessed grief separates you from love and the ability to attend to your Soul. Love is the highest vibration of existence. You are love. Being disconnected from love becomes the root of your pain. To offer true love it's important to know your love and value yourself.

Humans believe grief or other unpleasant emotions should be avoided. It's as if we are entitled to constant happiness, seeking only positive experiences and feelings. The chase for this unrealistic way of life is keeping many people disconnected from self-love and inner peace. It is through suffering that you have the opportunity to heal, to evolve, and touch the depth of your Soul.

Grief is also confusing. We grieve for what has passed, for what we wish we had, or for the missing love within our hearts. Personal grief comes from the love we deny ourselves because we have blocked our heart. Although we do not welcome this type of grief, it may seem easier to manage a closed heart than the fear we must overcome to open our hearts and love. Relationships can be destroyed if we are inept or unwilling to handle negative emotions, especially grief. A typical coping mechanism is to develop emotional amnesia.

> Grief can be the garden of compassion. If you keep your heart open through everything, your pain can become your greatest ally in your life's search for love and wisdom.
> —Rumi

The capacity to be receptive to love comes from the compassionate understanding of suffering. We do not need to be entangled in the negative behaviors of others to remain kind, giving, able, and free. We can achieve this mastery of the heart by first offering kindness, love, and compassion to ourselves.

My client Marsha shared the struggles she had with her narcissistic mother. There was deep sorrow in the distant and detached look in Marsha's eyes while she recalled her story. She told me that she felt unloved, unheard, and unworthy growing up. Although these are also symptoms of an imbalanced Solar Plexus due to shame (Chapter 3), Marsha needed help with grieving the lost love of her mother. Her mother was still living, but Marsha wanted to move forward as if her mother were dead. She hoped to detach from her mom to dull the pain of love and long-ing in her heart. As we went through the energy healing and emotional exercises, she learned that letting go wasn't the prescription for her heal-ing. Instead, Marsha needed to accept, connect, and strengthen the true love she had for her mother even though her mother brought her pain.

Marsha was unable to justify her emotions of love in the face of her pain. It created a conflict between her mind and her heart. She thought she could protect herself from future pain by abol-ishing the feeling of love and keeping the remembrances of hurt at bay. By fall-ing out of love with her mother Marsha believed she would stop grieving. "If I don't love her, she can't hurt me." In actuality what happens is, "If I don't love her, I close my heart to love."

> You, yourself, as much as anybody in the entire universe, deserve your love and affection.
> —Buddha

The acknowledgement that Marsha could love her mom without nec-essarily engaging in her mom's manipulations or beliefs was a revelation to her. And a relief. That she could still hold love in her heart while also processing other emotions freed Marsha from internal conflict that caused emotional suffocation. Her healing had begun.

Marsha needed to work on self-love. To help her, I mirrored what I saw in her Soul. I spoke loving words to her—words that her mother had never uttered. I told Marsha she was beautiful and that she had much to offer to others. We discussed how her pres-ence mattered and what she offered the world was important. It was clear her heart was generous. Most importantly, I affirmed that the Creator made her full

> We accept the love we think we deserve.
> —Stephen Chbosky

of love and that she was completely loveable. She was the worthiest of all and that her Soul was perfect.

At first Marsha couldn't accept what I told her. She looked at me with skeptical eyes. But the more we spoke, the more she accepted my words of encouragement. She wept. A weeping heart is a cleansing heart. At one point, she asked, "But isn't it selfish to believe I'm the most worthy?" At that moment this 30-something woman turned into a child. She was conflicted in her belief that if she was indeed worthy, she would be taking worthiness from someone else. Her fear confirmed the negative energy from her mother that filled her with shame.

All of us are the most worthy. We are equal in value and worth. Owning the love that you are is not taking love away from anyone else. You are love. You were made with the right ingredients for everything you need in life, and you are perfect. Even your flaws are perfectly designed. You deserve love and if you cannot find unconditional love from another, you can learn to give it to your Self.

Emotional Workout

Breathing Exercise: The Heart Chakra's element is air. Deep breathing is a wonderful way to energize this area. Put your right palm in the center of your chest. Put you left palm on your 2nd Chakra, which is on your lower belly just below your navel. Don't be lazy with your hands. Let your palm feel the clothes or skin on your body. Connect fully with your hand and with intention. Breathe into the chest and feel your hand rise. With each inhale, breathe in deeply and imagine the color green flowing in through your nostrils. After you inhale, hold the breath for up to the count of seven. As you exhale, imagine the green color gently fading. Repeat four times.

Healing is grace and freedom in the purest form. Healing is love. God is love. It is not always easy to keep a heart open to receive and give love, but love is the answer. It dispels fear and it untangles the tightest emotional knots. One simple act of loving kindness can shatter years of pain. Love is in your Soul. Love never dies, it simply transforms. As we allow love and compassion to heal us, we experience the gentle caress of grace. Grace is what allows us to ease into transformation without guilt, fear, or shame. Grace offers freedom. With an open heart we can accept the healing power of love, and the changes in our relationships will be free of strife, anger, or resentment. As our hearts remain connected, grace eases the transformation of change. You may not physically be with the one you love, but you stay connected in the energy of love for eternity. To resist love is to shut down your heart, but even through pain, closing your heart is unnecessary and unhealthy.

Follow Your Heart

Anita is a woman in her late 40s. She came to me because she felt "the dark cloud" over her life. Everything in the past two years seemed to be going downhill, especially her career. For quite some time she had juggled her 9-to-5 corporate job as well as her side job decorating cookies and pastries. I could tell by the way she spoke that the artistic side job was her heart. She described the unique flair of henna designs that she hand-crafted on wedding cakes and cookies. She boasted of her former A-list clients in New York City and showed me a few of her unique designs. Anita was an expert in her craft.

> Let yourself be silently drawn by the strange pull of what you really love. It will not lead you astray.
> —Jaluluddin Rumi

But her business had dropped substantially in the past year and, concurrently, she was laid off from her corporate job. Adding to her problems, her mother was ill and required a good deal of care.

I asked Anita what she wanted in her life and career. I pressed her to find her genuine heart calling and to follow it. She was stymied because she was not getting return calls on interviews in the financial sector. I asked if this is what she truly wanted, and would she be happy to return to that job? For 30 minutes she tried to convince me that she was happy and the job was fine. I heard a list of reasons why and how the corporate world was good for her. But she was resisting her heart and we both knew it. She was afraid of rejection and failure to go for her dreams full-time. She feared for her financial security and the loss of everything if she didn't succeed. Aware of her talents, I knew Anita was gifted and she could be successful in her business. I encouraged her to open her heart and be grateful that she had the time to care for her mother. Although she couldn't see the larger perspective, she needed time to regroup and plan her strategy for her pastry decorating business. We got excited together and dreamed about her goals. We worked on her heart energy and the solar plexus to fortify and rebalance.

A few months later I read on social media that she had landed a great gig in the city decorating pastries for a major brand client. And then there was another. And another. I reached out to confirm my suspicions that she was going for her heart and enjoying success. Sure enough, she applied the energy of fear that was bogging her down and used it as courage to return to her passions. And it worked.

The only difference between success and failure is the courage to try. Fear keeps us from following our hearts until we learn to use fear as the guide to action. Don't allow fear to stop you from following your heart's lead. That's when you lose your way. You may not find the level of success you hoped for in your attempt, but there will be personal growth, pride, and great stories in trying. Everything happens for a divine reason if you have the courage to perceive life through your heart. Following your heart is the path to self-love and inner peace.

Courage allows you to follow your heart. If you act with courage, fear will never win. Courage acts out loud, moving beyond the limits of your mind, standing up for the love that is contained in your heart. Courage seeks the discomfort of transformation because it knows that change is the natural evolution of life. There is no death in change, only the possibility to evolve and to grow. The word *encourage* means to give hope, stimulate, or support. These attributes fuel courage to be the agent of change.

As you use courage as your guiding light, fear will continue to play its sneaky games in your mind. When the mind tries to control your life, reach into your heart to find the courage to lead your way. Life is incredibly short on earth. How you choose to experience it will determine your happiness.

Courage is a love affair with the unknown.
—Osho

Green is the color associated with movement. It means go and to proceed. It is also the color that corresponds to the Heart Chakra. Think of it as the "yes" of your heart. It's like a traffic light. Red is stop. Green is go. The mind is too often controlled by fear but the heart is controlled by love. If you follow the call of your Soul, you will flow in the green as if the traffic lights are lined up in your favor. You are cruising. When you feel the light turn yellow, it cautions you to slow down and proceed slowly. You have experienced what yellow feels like as the hesitation or pause in your heart. It's the feeling of caution. The red light tells you something isn't right. Don't close your heart, just stop and refocus your direction. Get back on the right road. Follow your heart and GO.

You don't chase green lights, but do follow their lead. Most people overthink and under-feel. When we close our hearts to feelings, we rely more on our mind to lead the way and lose touch with who we are and what our hearts need. The mind is a useful tool, but it should not determine your every move. You are not your mind. The heart is the gateway to happiness.

Use the heart to guide your Soul and to follow your divine purpose. Follow the traffic signs to help travel the fearless path to your destination.

Emotional Workout

Thinking vs. Feeling: This exercise will keep your heart energy open. Many people have learned to respond from their mind, but we want to learn how to respond from the heart. At times the heart wants things that don't make much sense to us or to others. When you are perplexed, or want to practice heart awareness, ask yourself two questions. 1) What do I think? and 2) How do I feel? Write your answers or say them to yourself. Be sure to say them out loud. You will begin to differentiate between the mind's response and your heart's response. When you catch yourself over-thinking, ask yourself how you feel. Again, practice on decisions, relationships, or other issues in your life.

Travel Your Heart

Bridges are products of genius, and they are too often taken for granted. Bridges connect one place to another without changing the landscape below. This is also the core concept of emotional healing. Healing is about connecting and integrating one part of us to another part without negatively affecting the internal landscape.

Traveling your heart is different from following your heart. We desire the guidance of our hearts to lead us to happiness and freedom. But on our daily journey, we must travel our hearts to stay connected and open to self-love. For example, we need to travel the emotional distance of fear in our minds to the safety of our human presence. The heart bridges feelings of grief to our shame. We need to connect our voice to the feelings of our guilt in order to speak the truth. The heart allows this communication to happen. We must be frequent travelers of the bridge of our hearts to access each aspect of our reality.

Think of the heart as the bridge between heaven and Earth. Between the body and Soul. It's where true universal consciousness is fostered and where enlightenment has an opportunity to blossom. These things don't happen in the mind, as many believe. They happen in the heart. Your Soul is already enlightened; you are just opening your heart to connect back into your highest calling. Full awakening or spiritual evolvement happens when the heart has connected to the Soul. This is God calling and a reminder of our eternal home while we remain present in the physical world.

The heart speaks for the desires of our earthly bodies. We should honor these feelings and use them to understand the connection to our Soul, which includes the bigger picture of love. Agape love, the highest form of love, is an unconditional love that is beyond the limits of our minds. This is possible when the heart acts as the bridge, between the two worlds of body and Soul.

Life's journey is tough. We are not immune to experiences such as death of loved ones, divorce, or the loss of a job. Loss can hurt so much that the pain becomes intolerable. The focus is then on making the pain go away instead of honoring what pain teaches us. No longer are we connected to our genuine feelings (of pain) and allowing it to process, but we shift our focus on separating from the pain. We expect our hearts to function as a drawbridge on demand. When we choose, the roadway across the heart becomes disconnected, so that the emotional pathways from mind to body are not accessible.

The Attic

When I made the decision to leave Los Angeles to work on my emotional health and anxiety, I had my tail between my legs. I didn't know what I wanted or where I was going. I was defeated and tired. I knew I wanted to feel better and more like the spiritual, happy young woman who was a leader in her community and her life. So, I went home to Kentucky to

Emotional Workout

Heart Opener: Lie face-down on the floor. Put your forehead or your chin on the floor, bend your elbows, and place your palms down under your shoulders. Your fingertips should be in alignment with your upper chest, elbows pointed to the sky, toes lying flat with your back extended. On the inhale and using your lower back and core muscles, lift your chest off the floor. Your hands are there to assist, but not to push your entire body weight up. Your eyes gaze forward. Allow your heart to shine toward the ceiling. As you inhale, expand your heart, and as you exhale, gently return to the floor. Inhale and exhale here, then repeat. This heart opener is also a wonderful strengthening exercise for your torso and back.

regroup. I felt safe there. I needed to find peace and healing. I needed a direction for my life.

I moved into the attic of a friend's Victorian house in downtown Louisville. For the next nine months I slept on a futon and took long walks in the beautiful parks nearby. I sought help from therapists, healers, churches, organic farms, and sweat lodges. I tried anything I could do to feed my Soul and stoke the dream of a media and wellness career. Although Kentucky wasn't the best place for me to pursue my career, I knew it was important to stay long enough to stabilize myself and determine the best course of action. I needed this time to work through my fears.

While in Louisville, I volunteered at a local organization that fed the hungry on Thanksgiving Day. The vibe of the place was extremely festive, like Thanksgiving wrapped in Christmas. Everyone was happy and welcoming; the music was merry and the place was bustling. I was thrilled to be part of it all. Somewhere between the kitchen and the dining hall I spotted a handsome man running trays. His smile lit up the entire building. He hustled about serving meals, whistling, and making everyone feel special. He was full of charm.

I caught his eye and for the next two years we were magically engulfed in the flames of love. This relationship, albeit tumultuous and heartbreaking, was the spark that catapulted me into the next phase of my life. It was my "Right of Passion," the experience that blew open the doors of my closed heart.

Heath was easy to love. He had a child-like heart, and we laughed and played together like kids. The intimacy was amazing. I loved his humility and openness to talk about his feelings. Or so I thought. Every day I discovered new things about Heath, like the fact he still had a home in Atlanta. I knew he worked there on occasion, but soon our romance became part-time due to his commute.

I felt so lucky to find a man I was crazy about, along with the healing my Soul was longing for. Life's possibilities seemed endless and jolted me out of my prior anxiety state and into action. Within months, I moved to Nashville to share a house with him and start a new life.

I had been in love before, but there was something special about this relationship. It was more than the feeling of love for another. It was like standing on the edge of a precipice and a part of me was about to be freed, to soar and fly.

The chemistry was electric and we shared common interests, but as time went along, something wasn't right. On more than one occasion I felt the yellow light of caution in my heart.

As it turned out, Heath was married to a woman in Atlanta. He lied about it

The heart is the bridge between Heaven and Earth.

for months. He was addicted to sex and he juggled numerous relationships at once. I hung in there for a while, in disbelief. The situation was so confusing; I couldn't sort through it all. In the end, I was angry, hurt, and devastated. The last time I saw Heath was in the back of a police car on the Upper West Side of Manhattan. He had made too many wrong choices that left him broke, distraught, and caught in his web of lies.

I have no regrets. This hurtful relationship spurred me to move to Manhattan and it ultimately set me on the path to the life I wanted. It was the first time that love broke my heart wide open. It ripped through the padlocks that chained me to previous grief and to my fear of self-love. It was the bridge I needed to get back in touch with my Soul. The flame of our love didn't last, but the experience became the torch that guided me back to my Soul path.

Every part of your past has meaning. There is a purpose and reason for every hurt, every love, and every experience. And it happens at the right time whether we are aware of it or not. A sage heart knows that beyond the wishes of your mind or the force of your will, there is a greater plan. It is your Soul's plan. This is faith in process.

Self-love means integrating and accepting what life offers you. When you hurt, take time to feel and heal. When you are happy, share hope with others and prepare your mind and heart for new experiences. The ocean of life brings forth constant waves, with some serene and others large and intense.

Emotional Workout

Date Night: Take yourself on a date this week. There's nothing that opens your heart more than a little personal TLC. Resist the urge to invite others. The time alone may seem unusual or uncomfortable, but try it. Don't go shopping or pay bills. Do something enjoyable like going to dinner at a nice restaurant. Dress up. See a movie or eat a gourmet ice cream cone on a bench in the park. Love yourself generously.

If you have a wounded heart, find a safe space surrounded by nature and friends. Think of a place where you can tune out the world and rest. This is not to escape, but to gain strength of heart to be open to what life has in store for you. Find the place that gives you a new perspective on life. It could be a fairy-tale romance or the loss of a job that may unleash the chains of your fear, which will break your heart open. Follow your heart and love again.

I Don't Like It, but I Allow It

Allowing an emotion to surface doesn't mean you like it or that the action that caused the emotion is justified. There's no judgment with your healing process. Allowing emotion simply stops the resistance to it, which stops the internal conflict. If there is no resistance, there is no conflict. Resistance forces us to harbor feelings, creating a heavy and burdensome dark cloud over us.

Connect to your authentic feelings by changing your pattern. You are the only person who knows how you feel. You are only harming yourself by hiding or denying your emotion. You don't help or save another from pain. Remember: You are not responsible for how another person feels or responds to life. You are responsible only for your actions and your feelings. If you harm another person, you are responsible for owning those actions, but not for their response.

The healing cycle is 1) you feel pain; 2) you allow it; and 3) you process the healing. If you cause pain, you should own it to allow healing to begin. It's the cycle of love and forgiveness. You can't escape pain, but you can move through it with less self-imposed suffering if you participate in its healing cycle.

You may not like an emotion, but if you allow it, you'll see the emotion will soon change. The more you stay connected to it the quicker the emotional charge will weaken. By being present with the emotion and allowing it to be what it is, the internal conflict is gone. It just "is." Reality turns your metaphorical lights on to reveal the pain you were trying to hide. Fear is never as scary with the lights on. If you detach and stay in the dark, the emotion will run wild and try to control your whole existence. Unattended emotions become scary monsters. Be present with yourself and the emotion will soften. Connection is the path to all healing.

Vulnerability is required to open. Love and heartache are what we fear, but experiencing these emotions is the path to healing. Hug people. Forgive yourself. Find compassion for someone that has harmed you. Smile more. Cry. Laugh. Be honest with how you feel.

Dismissing any emotion is dangerous. Emotions are alive and communicate important information to our minds and bodies. We are wired to comprehend and gauge life by emotion. At a moment's notice we can experience happiness or anger, guilt or sadness. All emotions are part of our constitution. Changing our thoughts can change a negative or habitual pattern, but it won't rid us of the emotion or our vulnerability to it. Resisting a feeling or attempting to "let go" is to fight against ourselves by not honoring the natural flow of life.

As we mature and evolve, we expand our capacity for emotional consciousness. Every circumstance and each person are different because there are no two emotions exactly alike. Emotions are as unique as each of us, yet they are universal in language. We all know sadness. But sadness from the loss of two different friends may feel like two different emotions. The feeling is specific to the energy it is connected to, whether it's a person, event, place, work, or any other experience. To identify your feelings, you must be willing to experience and connect to them. Otherwise a path to healing will be difficult.

Heart Chakra Basics

Color: Green

Gemstones: Emerald, Unakite, Rose Quartz, Jade, Green Calcite

Essential Oils: Geranium, Jasmine, Ylang Ylang, Lavender, Bergamot, Neroli, Orange, Rose, Eucalyptus, Pine, Sandalwood

Meditation

Close your eyes and take a deep breath. Feel the seat or the ground you're sitting on. As you breathe, imagine that a gentle relaxation is washing over you that opens your muscles and arteries. Your whole body is becoming more at ease. Breathe into your chest and notice your emotions. Perhaps you are struggling with an issue. Maybe you harbor jealousy or resentment. On your next inhale, allow your emotion to come fully into your presence. Notice how it feels. Does your chest feel tight? Are you fearful? Are you resisting and tightening the muscles in your face or your arms? Allow your feelings. Soften your body with the breath.

Imagine that you can see an emotion like jealousy inside your body. What does it look like? What color is it? What shape does it take? Where does the emotion live or hide in your body? Breathe with it until you can describe its nature.

As you breathe, use this mantra: "I allow." It's important to not act on the feeling or get involved; you are simply being present to the emotion and observing. You are allowing it to be. That doesn't mean you like it, but you allow it. The less you resist, the less it persists.

Spiritual Mapping

Use a blank sheet of paper and a pen. In the middle of the paper, make a circle or dot and name it "Heart." We're going to track your journey from suffering to love.

Think of a feeling or situation that you struggle with at the present. Give the issue a name. An example is loneliness. Yours may be anger or resentment, grief or jealousy. Find a name that associates with your emotional struggle and use it for this practice.

Next, give a reference point to your issue, considering time and space. Using the sheet of paper as a relative scale of life, write down your struggle that is relative to the distance from your heart. For example, if you've felt loneliness all your life, put the mark for loneliness at the edge of your page, farthest away from the Heart. Write "Loneliness" next to the mark. If it's a very recent issue, put it an inch or two away from the Heart mark.

Between the Heart and the word that marks your suffering, place at least three (for shorter distances) or up to 10 marks. Your map will start to look like a trail. Starting with your issue and working back to your Heart, write an outline in chronological order of actions, reactions, or circumstances that have caused your suffering. Use insight and honesty.

This exercise does not place blame or responsibility on others. It is a tool for self-growth rather than justifying your role as a victim. For example, my marks may be:

1. My spouse works all the time.
2. My reaction to spouse working is to stay home instead of engage with friends.
3. I extricate myself from groups or activities that I could participate in.
4. I don't feel like I fit in.
5. Too much private time isn't healthy for me.
6. I like alone time.
7. I need love.

Start with your heart to track how you get from an open heart to a closed heart of suffering. In the example, I recognize that I need love, but I like my alone and private time. But too much doesn't feel good. In the fear that I don't fit in, I don't go out in the world. I hide behind my fear and choose unavailable men, which keeps me alone. I was the co-creator in my story of loneliness, and I hide my suffering there.

Your map or tracking will only make sense to *you* and that's fine. The point is to show the role you play in your reality that is keeping you from happiness and peace. It will highlight where you are detached and the loop that you are living in. I kept replaying feelings of loneliness. My resolve was "If I stay true to my heart and not hide behind fear, I can be with someone who is available. I just need some alone time." To connect back to my heart connects me to my real feelings that I want and need love.

CHAPTER 5

Declare

Your words will either give you joy or give
you sorrow, but if they were spoken without
regret, they will give you peace.

—Shannon L. Alder

Your voice is an important barometer of your health. Like a finely tuned instrument, it reveals emotions such as fear, joy, strength and shame. What is said and how it is said are testimony to inner harmony. With minor nuance in tone, pace, or inflection, the voice reveals character and personality as well as mental and emotional health. An emotional imbalance will manifest in the throat or physical movement as weakness, restriction, or unevenness. Hoarseness or a "frog" in the throat is a sign of an internal emotional struggle.

Before language or advanced intellect humans conveyed information with sound and movement. Grunts and utterances delivered feelings and information from the mind and body. Over the centuries man has developed more sophisticated techniques to communicate, helping us evolve into high-functioning and manipulative beings. The ability to stay connected to self and others comes from tools of communication, be it speech or movement. It is by this same means that we distance and disconnect ourselves from others.

The power of expression can influence one person, a group or the entire world. Articulate leaders have inspired millions to follow their lead with a passionate conviction for good or evil. Activists and social justice groups influence massive change and evolution through the passion of their voice and conviction of their heart. Words unsaid are often equally powerful. Finding the genuine and appropriate voice for yourself is a balancing act.

The voice should be used as a tool for expressing thought and emotion, not as a means of control. Poor communication skills can be damaging to self and others. Constriction or restriction of the voice may appear due to yelling, lying, diminishing others, or negative talk to self or others. The fear to speak up or express your needs can also have a detrimental effect.

Barbara and Bill were "the perfect couple." Affluent and educated, with beautiful children and a lovely home, they were the classic example of success. Bill was a politician for more than 30 years and Barbara served as the committed politician's wife. The power-duo and their children were known and respected in their mid-sized, conservative town. They were role models in their community. People admired their family life, their strong religious beliefs and their commitment to their work. To many, they symbolized the American dream.

I met Barbara and Bill when I lived in California. Barbara was a kind, jovial, and down-to-earth woman. I enjoyed her company and demeanor. Bill was smart and friendly, but his over-zealous personality was a problem.

He acted like the world was his stage and it was impossible to hold a conversation with him. He was used to commandeering the conversation in most any setting. I sensed that Barbara struggled with Bill's behavior. He talked over her, spoke for her, or talked so much that Barbara had no chance to voice her opinions or thoughts. In social situations, she would simply smile and play the role of the supportive wife.

During their marriage Bill had an affair, yet Barbara remained loyal and commitment to him through it all. Barbara, ever present and strong, did her best to rise above the incident and continue her support and love for her husband.

Years later Barbara requested a healing session with me. She was in town and hoped to reconnect and do some personal self-care. When she walked through the door, Barbara was beautiful as ever, but her spirit looked dim, tired, and less vibrant than I recalled. In her mid-50s, she had physically aged, but it was the emotional wear that I detected on her face.

After a big hug, we sat down to talk. Barbara's voice crackled and was barely audible when she spoke. It was difficult to hear her. When I asked about her voice, she shared that she had developed a rare vocal cord problem that caused strain and some loss of her voice. Although there was little danger in her medical prognosis, the problem was irreversible and she had little hope of improvement, which meant she faced difficulty in speaking for the rest of her life.

Knowing Barbara's personality and history, I was careful to not jump to conclusions about her emotional health. I allowed Barbara to guide our session for a while as she told me about her life and her health. After discussing the usual and superficial issues that surfaced, I asked about Bill. Her body shifted, then she smiled as she rattled off his recent accomplishments. As we delved deeper into the subject her vocal problem became the focal point of my attention.

Barbara's voice had been stifled for years. In light of the difficult and personal hardships, she took the "high road" as she called it, not dealing with personal issues in public. She kept her opinions and thoughts to herself in support of her family's image. Over time she learned that being quiet and submissive to Bill made their home life easier as well.

Over the years she never discussed her personal heartbreak of her husband's affair, or the years she was verbally shut down in social situations. Barbara believed expressing her feelings meant that she would be shaming her husband. She loved him through thick and thin, and she thought she was effectively dealing with his domineering personality. Little did she know her silence cost her the health of her voice.

Barbara's story is not uncommon. Both women and men have the potential to lose their voice as fear of expressing oneself often overrides one's truth. Sometimes it happens literally, other times metaphorically. Shame, embarrassment and a host of other reasons cause the inability to speak with integrity, confidence, and authenticity.

The Throat Chakra

The 5th or Throat Chakra is the Communications Center. It's also called The Seat of Emotion. Healthy energy in this area coincides with speaking one's truth and giving expression to desires, wants, needs, opinions, and thoughts. As the first of the higher vibration spiritual chakras, this energy center demands the highest integrity and authentic truth that is often challenged by self-doubt and negative thinking. The Throat Chakra is more than simple vocal expression. It also includes body language, written expression, and how we understand the expression of others. When the Throat Chakra is out of balance, there is often another emotional energy system that needs attention. The primary blockages to a healthy Throat Chakra are the untruths we tell ourselves and others. Deceit, lies, and manipulation are the blocks that keep us trapped.

Physical symptoms that may arise from an unhealthy Throat Chakra are below. Do not discount the importance of these issues. If they are persistent, please seek the help of a physician.

Gum or teeth issues	Hoarseness
Neck pain	Dental issues
Clearing of throat	Polyps on glands
Chronic fatigue	TMJ
Headaches	Hearing issues
Thyroid and endocrine issues	Difficulty swallowing
Sore throat	Vocal constriction

Ignoring our fears or shortcomings traps energy in our body and can develop into a variety of other emotional symptoms and patterns.

Gossiping	Fear of public speaking
Fear of ridicule or judgment	Dominating conversations
Shyness	Verbal outbursts
Stubbornness	Deceitfulness
Verbal abuse	Arrogance
Manipulation	Afraid to speak up
Inability to express thoughts	Resentments
Social anxiety	Poor listener

The Truth About Lies

It's interesting that as we grow up we learn that lies are not acceptable, no matter their size. But we also absorb the opposite message which is to not reveal the truth. It's to our detriment that our parents and teachers didn't encourage us to speak our real feelings or opinions in a healthy way. The truth is our personal feelings and beliefs reveal who we are. There is no person or opinion that can negate your truth.

We lie as a measure of protection. Lying covers a truth that we don't want revealed for various reasons. The personal lies that we tell others and ourselves hide origins to our pain and suffering that we often do not want to admit. We lie because we are afraid to say who we are. To reveal our true nature is to risk rejection. We fear ridicule and embarrassment in exposing our true self, because we see ourselves as flawed and our weaknesses are hard to accept.

In seeking attention, children learn to manipulate and lie to get what they want. They also learn to stifle their voice to please a loved one. We learn at an early age that telling lies help us avoid the shame we feel in expressing our genuine feelings or desires. Children hushed from an early age may carry that energy into adulthood and shy away from full expression of self. Or they may become the tattle-tale in the group. If a person can't say what they see or how they feel without getting themselves into trouble or feeling shame, they tell on their sibling or friend. Tattle-tales expose the secrets and lies of others and get a bad rap from not being "cool" enough to hide the truth. The tattle-tales are then avoided or shunned by their peers.

Expressing our emotions is difficult, as most of us were taught as children to be quiet. Many people grew up being shamed for their voice. These people may grow to develop difficulty in asserting themselves in a career or relationship. It's common for parents to hush their children. "Speak only when you're spoken to," or "Don't talk back," or "Be polite," are messages parents use to admonish their children. Adults also receive verbal or nonverbal messages on how to behave. It's easy to become trapped behind the rules of society about what we should say, what we should wear, and how we should feel. Men feel ashamed to display their sensitive emotions because they don't want to appear weak. Men are then blamed for not being sensitive enough. Woman are scorned for displaying too much emotion or too little emotion, making them seem difficult to please, cold, or abrasive. To make matters worse, many people espouse philosophies such as "let it go" or "be calm," suggesting these are the best routes to happiness.

You can't be calm and happy by chasing calm and happy. Peace doesn't ensue because you make the peace sign. Happiness and peace follow the acceptance and expression of your genuine feelings and the connection to who you are. The emotional healing process is a sign of self-love, which creates peace.

I am not an advocate for displaying inappropriate anger, anxiety, or other negative emotions, but it is important to voice your true, authentic emotions. There's a vast difference.

I asked my friend Josh if there was anything that he was afraid of. He said no. When I pressed the issue, he owned up to his fears but said he would send them to me by email. He didn't want to talk about them. Josh didn't have typical adult fears such as the loss of his career or of death. His fears emanated from his childhood. He was afraid of dolls and clowns. He believed these fears appeared because his older brother had tormented him in his youth. Josh wouldn't share his feelings because he was too embarrassed to admit such juvenile, silly fears.

Depending on your background, support system, and environment, fears can be the hardest things to admit and emotionally handle. I received another email from a man in a nearby town, inquiring about healing sessions. Dave called himself a "tough guy with anxiety" and proceeded to spill his heart about his life-long struggle with panic, fears, and phobias. He described himself as a stereotypical New Jersey Italian tough guy who was debilitated by his issues. At one time, the anxiety became so intense he became agoraphobic. The only thing bigger than his fear was his shame. He couldn't maintain his tough guy persona if he admitted his condition to his family or friends. When he was growing up he learned that talking about such things made him appear weak, or at least that was his perception. He suffered needlessly for years and continues to struggle. As we talked it was apparent that his treatment program did not address the root of his emotions. The treatment just addressed the symptoms.

One successful healing strategy Dave now uses is to focus his energy on helping others as a drug and alcohol counselor. He provides a caring and safe environment for "tough guys" like criminals and addicts as they work through their struggles.

Shame or embarrassment should not be connected to any emotion. Concealing one's feelings and denying who you are is only damaging to one person: you. It is your responsibility to have healthy and honest expressions. Learn to say what you mean and mean what you say.

One of the main reasons we lie is to hide our pain and suffering. When asked how we are, we respond with "fine" or "okay." It's become common practice to guard one's expression as a means of being courteous to others or not airing dirty laundry. But it's not fine. Continual use of these lies keeps us farther away from our happiness and healing.

It's not just deceit and lies that contribute to the imbalance of our unhealthy expression. Addiction is another indicator that emotional healing is needed. You can't be harmonious with yourself and be in addiction. To deny that truth is to lie to yourself. When I smoked, I lied to myself about my emotional and physical health. After years of being hooked, I lied so much it became humorous. When I smoked, I convinced myself I was meditating or having some sort of spiritual experience alone in the great outdoors. I wanted to believe smoking connected me to my ancestry of the American Indian culture. The truth was the buzz from the smoke was covering the volcano of emotions that were deep in my body. It was my smoke screen.

The "vice" du jour offers a moment of pleasure or relief from the pain that we try to avoid. But the negative behavior is just a vice grip on your troubled inner world. It holds your suffering and it won't let go.

Emotional Workout

Breathe and Release: This is simple exercise for times filled with stress or tension. When you notice internal tension, take three deep inhales and exhales from the nose. Be steady in breathing, and do not go too fast. Imagine each inhale traveling deeper into your body, freeing jammed emotions. On the fourth round, inhale through your nose and exhale through your mouth, making sounds, moans, words, or expressions that need to be released. Do not judge or restrict sounds that your body wants to make. Practice up to three rounds.

What blocks your expression to others? Keeping secrets can be due to an internal conflict. In your journal, list three things that you do not feel comfortable voicing to another person.

The lies we tell ourselves mask the truth of our integrity. Carrying such shame and fearing to admit the truth of our suffering is difficult even to ourselves. Perhaps we chase false dreams, but to ignore dreams confirms the feelings of worthlessness. Perhaps you are in denial about an eating disorder or addiction. You may be lying about your true feelings about your spouse or a friendship. These personal lies become internalized as self-criticism, self-loathing or denial of self-love. We are afraid to judge ourselves so we create excuses, blame others, and manipulate situations to avoid the hurt. We lie to avoid infliction of self-pain to our spirit. Name two lies that you hide behind or ways that you are not honest with yourself.

What Is Your Truth?

Let's talk about your truth. Expressing your truth comes through self-love and acceptance. If you can't accept your past, you cannot tell your truth.

It's surprising how often we are not truthful with ourselves. It's due to the disconnection between our true self and our pain. There's a multitude of events in our daily lives that require our input. Without careful consideration, we respond in a way that placates or distracts from the actual truth. Food is a good example. How many times do you eat because you tell yourself you are hungry? The truth is you may be bored, sad, angry, or lonely. Food becomes a fill-in and a distraction from the truth. Rather than eat, you should attend to your boredom (likely a 2nd Chakra imbalance) and find something creative to do. Or address your loneliness. If you don't feel confident to be yourself or take the time to listen within, self-manipulation may become part of your routine. This scenario can take place in different types of situations such as financial or career decisions, relationships, and in our spirituality. Often the response "I don't know" is used when we disconnect from ourselves. "I don't know" is akin to "I'm fine." It is laziness mixed with the fear of your truth.

The more your truth is hidden the more you position yourself to suffer in the future. Children need lessons and positive role modeling to learn how to express their hurt feelings at home or on the playground. Without these lessons, their anger as adults may turn into rage with the slightest trigger. People with this behavior are called bullies. There's no mystery to people who bully, they are just people who have unprocessed residual emotions that have brewed into an emotional storm. This is an example of how unprocessed feelings can become dangerous. When you lie about how you feel, the opportunity to live your truth and to be happy is lost. Lies never win, but the truth endures.

Three things cannot be long hidden; the sun, the moon, and the truth.
—Buddha

Telling the truth is the way to real and honest expression. Anything less than that creates imbalances and problems. Anger expressed appropriately is less likely to develop into rage. The acceptance of any emotion will often dissipate its energy and keep it from escalating. You do not need to act on every emotion, but always be honest in what you feel. Being authentic will lessen the hurt to self and others. It is not the emotion we should fear, it is the denial of fear that is dangerous.

It's not your responsibility to decide how other people respond to you, how they act, or how they feel about you. Your only responsibility is to be honest and genuine with yourself. Healing has nothing to do with another person. What anyone else does or says is their responsibility, even if it is directed toward you. It is up to you how you respond to and utilize an experience. Your healing is your responsibility.

Meeting and talking with people are opportunities to practice your authenticity. When someone asks you how you are doing, try to respond with some thought and then share your feelings with the person. When someone asks you what you do for a living, be creative in your description of who you are and what excites you about getting up in the morning. For example, telling someone you are an engineer only provides a job title, rather than explaining what you do with your time and talent. In being more forthcoming to others, you may find that people are fascinated with your world.

Emotional Workout

Speak It: Try this in a safe or private space. Say how you feel. Use your voice, words, and even body gestures to describe it. Do not judge; do not filter. "I feel so hurt that she forgot my birthday." "I've never been so happy in my life!" "I'm ashamed that I cheated." Whatever you feel, speak it.

Cody has two healthy children, a dog, and a lovely home. But she's unhappy in her marriage. As a symptom of their discontent, she and her husband haven't had sex in 10 years due to a constant undercurrent of strife. He won't bring up their issues, and she is too afraid to take action and upset the children; they are her priority. Even though she's unhappy and unfulfilled, she hasn't been able to speak to him directly about their problems or how she feels. She doesn't want to disturb the household or upset him.

Over time, Cody begins to find things wrong with her husband. She looks for ways to blame him as an excuse to rationalize her own feelings. If he is the one in the wrong, or if she can place focus on his inadequacies, it gives her a reason to not want to be with him any longer. This allows Cody to avoid the blame she would feel in breaking up her family. Her personal feelings do not provide her with enough justification or rationalization to feel safe and confident in her future. She needs an exterior reason to hide behind her authentic feelings because she isn't confident enough to believe her emotions are valid and meaningful.

As time goes on almost everything her husband does starts to get under her skin. She finds his lack of certain skills deplorable. She knows that she's being negative about her husband, but her need is strong to create more justification of her feelings. She continues focusing on his faults and calling out his shortcomings. Recently she had verbal outbursts and called him stupid. After a trivial incident, she became so frustrated that she yelled, "I'm done with this relationship!"

Of course, her verbal attacks and outbursts were shocking and hurtful to her husband. He recoiled in his shame.

Cody then feels ashamed of her actions. In an effort to redeem her husband's feelings and save face, she does an about-face and goes in for the rescue. She apologizes and denies that she meant any of her words. This passive-aggressive behavior reinforces the dysfunctional cycle of their relationship. Neither of them is emotionally healthy or mature enough to say how they feel, so they dance around power and abuse in effort to control their emotions. It is likely that neither of them will own up to what is needed to promote healing. They both use their fear to stay stuck. The fear of their truth, fear of change, fear of loneliness, and fear of failing as parents to avoid making changes in their lives.

This is a real-life story I've heard many times. People get stuck in the loop of fear and it inhibits the expression of their real feelings. It is also a reason to blame others as a way to validate oneself. Instead of accepting and acting responsibly, we find excuses of blame or negative behaviors in another person to hide our own feelings. Guilt and shame have the capacity to overcome us, yet we don't say how we feel.

Emotional Workout

Mirror Work: Stand or sit in front of a mirror and look yourself in the eyes. Take some time to get comfortable, as this simple process may bring up emotions and insecurities. During the next three to five minutes, have a conversation with yourself in the mirror. Say what you are feeling and say what you need or want. Try to maintain eye contact and look with compassion and self-love. There is no shame or judgment in your feelings. Allow them to be free.

Speaking Your Truth

We know that our emotional wellness and happiness includes the acceptance of what life offers. This acceptance allows us to utilize the energy of our true emotions to meet life's challenges. We must accept grief, as well as shame. We may not like it but we allow it. Don't deny grief or use blame to remain a victim, instead deal effectively with your feelings in the moment. The next step is to speak your truth.

Being afraid is a healthy sign of growth. It signifies that we are active in our pursuits of transformation and things are about to change. It becomes a problem only if your fear immobilizes you. Speaking and behaving in authentic ways can cause anxiety if it's a new behavior for you, but being authentic will free you from the fear.

Speaking your truth brings the full responsibility for self into clear focus. Our lies are not necessary or rational, but to us, they often feel like the difference between life and death. Or love and rejection. A friend of mine is a brilliant artist and a regular contributor to the local and national art scene. He tells everyone that he is a Democrat but he's a closet Republican. He does this for acceptance. Most of his artist friends are more liberal than he is, and he has a need to be accepted amongst his peers. The fear of being rejected is bigger for him than the freedom to be authentic.

When you lie, play the victim and hide behind false realities, you feel trapped. It becomes easier to continue hiding behind the shame, depression or false identity than to own and accept it in honesty and love.

When you are clear and confident about who you are, you will own your true self and what goes on in your life. This ownership allows you to stay connected and work through your healing. There is no one to blame or image to cling onto. There's no projection or cycle of shame. If you do not hide behind shame or false images, you shorten the distance between your dreams and the realization of a new life.

> Fear is a natural reaction to moving closer to the truth.
> —Pema Chodron

The truth sets you free but it is often the freedom that frightens people.

When you are free you may choose what to do, what to wear, and where to live. You create your life. Freedom is alluring, but the reality of becoming free is challenged by fears of our weaknesses. When the door to freedom opens, we must have the courage to walk through it, or our reality doesn't change. It's only the fear of change that manipulates your mind into non-action.

Blocking the expression of pain also blocks the voice of your pleasure. It's unreasonable to concentrate only on the positive parts of life. Some ideologies recommend not to speak or think in a negative way for fear of manifesting a negative reality. This example of false teaching keeps us disconnected from our truth. I know a woman who refuses to talk about any type of negative stressor. If you mention them in front of her, she silences you by saying "Dismiss that" or "Retract!" She is playing mind games that keep her trapped in fear. Refusing to say the words "I need a root canal" won't make the need for the root canal go away. In fact, it keeps us from attending with great care to the courage and resources needed to prepare for getting the dental care we need. Don't discount your feelings or the reality of life. There's a great difference in speaking the truth versus dwelling in negativity or playing victim. Speaking truth creates a balance between the positive and the negative. The truth is, you can't have the yin without the yang, the light without the darkness, or the positive without the negative. To speak truth is to accept this reality and harness its energy. You cannot cherry-pick the positive out of life by ignoring the negative.

Be Who You Are

Part of self-expression is claiming your originality. You are unique and special, and you should tell the world who you are! One of the good ways social media has helped our culture is to encourage originality. People like to be voyeurs and experience the world through the eyes of others. We're fascinated with how other people live their lives. I believe this intrigue helps us become more empathetic and accepting of others, and with ourselves. Watching others make mistakes frees us to accept our own mistakes. In the eyes of authenticity and originality, there is nothing more perfect than imperfection. Your struggles can help others accept their own. We rely on each other, to confirm we are not alone and that our negative self-shame can be freed.

As you speak from your heart and from your Soul, remember that although you are not responsible for how others behave or feel, you are responsible to speak with integrity and respect. Saying who you are or how you feel should not be detrimental to others. What you say may bring uncomfortable issues to light, but it's possible to avoid blaming, harmful or derogatory terms, and hurt if you speak with integrity. Integrity supports your wholeness by using truth and high moral standards to deliver your expression.

Emotional Workout

Chanting: If you aren't familiar or practiced in yoga or similar traditions, chanting may feel awkward at first. Allowing discomfort is part of the healing. Find a phrase, prayer, or mantra to vocalize and chant. Start with the simple "Om," considered a sacred sound and mantra in many traditions, or the name of God or another spiritual connotation. Inhale, and as you exhale, open your mouth and give sound to your phrase. If it's a single syllable, hold the sound throughout the exhale and feel the vibration in your chest and around your lips. This practice is best done before or after meditation, after yoga, or as a vocal energizer before performances of any kind. Chanting aligns our spirit to Soul, opens our energy channels, and energizes our connection to the divine. It's a beneficial practice for attaching truth to sound or thought. It is also said to reduce anxiety and relieve depression.

I once hired a marketing consultant in New York City to help launch my new video series. He made bold claims of what he could do for my company by generating publicity. As a young entrepreneur who was shooting for the stars, I hung on his every word. But months later, my business growth remained stagnant. He did manage to throw a big party in the city on my behalf. More than 500 people came to celebrate the launch of my business. Clearly he was good at throwing parties. At the event, I circulated and did the host thing, while he and his staff worked the door, collected email addresses for our newsletter, gave out gifts, and served drinks. It was a great night.

After the event, I asked for the list of attendees and their email addresses. Increasing visibility is huge in media, and the emails collected at the party were to become one of my biggest assets. He dismissed me for several weeks, claiming different excuses. Sadly, I was conned. The people he hired to work my party worked for another company who were in cahoots with my marketing consultant. The staff who collected names was doing so under false pretenses. The names were going to a nightclub outlet that threw parties for corporate companies in the city and needed a fresh list of prospects.

I didn't receive the list and he didn't get paid. He made every excuse possible as to what happened with the emails, but I didn't believe a word from his mouth. A few months later, he sued me. In court, I spoke my truth, without reacting to his lies, and delivered my testimony with integrity. It was an easy win.

There's always a benefit when you speak with integrity and own your life. The reward may not be what you expect but it's often better. From that experience I learned the power of the truth. I learned that my voice mattered and I shouldn't pay for unfulfilled promises. There will always be people who try to blame you for their lies or wrong-doing, but you do not have to allow them to prevail. You are only responsible for standing your ground in your life and following the path that is right for you.

Other people's behavior is their business. Focus on how to empower your own life. You cannot expect someone else to be active in your healing or control your actions. Emotional healing is about owning the truth of who you are, what you feel, and how you will process and resolve those feelings so that you live free and happy. That's the responsibility of self. There's nothing selfish about it. It is the most productive way to use your energy, and the more free and happy you are, the more everyone gains.

If you are still unable to own your experiences, you can be confident that more healing is needed. Making excuses for your life or blaming others for things that didn't go in your favor is part of denial. Playing the victim in any capacity is a sign that self-love and healing are needed. It is your job, and yours only, to own and work on recovering and reconnecting to emotional health.

In addition to problems with self-expression, other areas may also be revealed by the Throat Chakra. For example, if you feel unsafe in your environment, you may have Root energy blockage causing anxiety and fear. It is impossible to know who you are if you don't have the fundamental foundation of safety. If you are creatively blocked and not expressing your passions and desires, the throat area may be blocked because of stagnant energy flow in the Sacral Chakra. If you lie to yourself or others, it will be revealed in your energy, tone, or in the throat. Physical restrictions or twitches are likely to develop in the repression of blocked energy.

You are either speaking your creativity, shame, grief, or guilt, or you are suppressing these emotions. Authentic expression requires you to attend to the areas that are afflicted with pain. This is the true definition of owning your truth. And your Throat Chakra will reveal the truth or the imbalance.

Some people have a fear of public speaking. It can develop into a phobia if the underlying issues are not addressed. Performing either reveals a person's self-confidence or hidden issues of shame and guilt. Performance anxiety can cause the voice to stutter, or become weak or small, or the voice will shut off completely. The neck may stiffen; the body may sweat or anxiety might take over. Others have no problem expressing themselves on stage or in front of a camera, yet they may suffer in personal and vulnerable exchanges like the sharing of their heart. Some may develop a shyness that covers their self-worth, or fear of love or intimacy. How we express ourselves in public or private can be quite different. As we start to untangle the suffering and heal properly, we begin to feel the freedom to express who we are, what we want, and our authentic truth.

Listening

Communication goes beyond speaking and expressing who we are. Communication also includes listening. We often hear people speak words yet we do not listen to what they say. Or, we are listening selfishly, waiting to respond with judgments or with our own viewpoint on the matter. We want to impart our knowledge but we have a hard time accepting the voice of reason from another. Being present and just listening can be challenging. There is a subtle fear that arises in the process of listening, and that fear keeps many of us at arms-length from relationships.

When you listen deeply without judgment or selfishness, you will receive lots of information. You will hear emotion and sense the energy of a person's experience. This can be uncomfortable. What you hear may challenge your beliefs, make you feel threated or affect your own feelings. You may hear that the person needs attention or love that you are afraid to give. What they say may reveal aspects of your own behavior that are uncomfortable to face. Are you willing to accept what you hear? Can you allow others to speak their truth, however different from yours, and truly hear what they have to say?

> So when you are listening to somebody, completely, attentively, then you are listening not only to the words, but also to the feeling of what is being conveyed, to the whole of it, not part of it.
> —Jiddu Krishnamurti

Good listening skills require patience and empathy. Empathy allows you to imagine the feelings and experiences of others. It's as if you share feelings with the person, without asserting your own. It's putting yourself in their shoes. Their perspective, frame of reference, and history are undoubtedly different than yours, but being empathetic allows the understanding of their truth. It's not up to you to like or deny what they say, it is only for you to witness, accept and try to understand. This is empathetic listening.

Deep listening can be challenging in a world of distractions and the desire to make everything rosy and positive. It's easier to pretend to listen while staying focused on your own agenda. But if you are interested in speaking your truth, listening completes the process. You become authentic by being present and participating in a relationship with self and others. We can only explore the world from our perspective for so long. Growth and knowledge are gained when we seek information beyond our culture and our personal belief system. Take responsibility for your own healing and speak your truth. Listen with empathy and intrigue to discover deeper parts of you that yearn to be revealed. This yearning is the call of your Soul. Your response is self-love.

Emotional Workout

Mini Vipassana: Vipassana is an insight meditation that cleanses the mind of thought and distractions that cause distress and pain. Devoted practitioners often retreat for several weeks at a time at certain locations. We will call this exercise a mini Vipassana, a Day of Silence and mindfulness. The effects are achieved by practicing present moment living and doing so in silence. You can practice for one day. Choose any day that will allow you to see the practice through. There will be no speaking or communication of any form. No electronics or texting. You may experience initial fear or anxiety, but challenge yourself to stay through the process. Choose to do things that are engaging in the present moment, such as walking in nature, meditating, or preparing nourishing meals. This is a wonderful mindfulness practice, and a time to listen to your inner truth while giving your voice a break!

Throat Chakra Basics

Color: Light Blue

Gemstones: Sodalite, Amazonite, Blue Calcite, Blue Lace Agate, Aquamarine, Lapis Lazuli, Turquoise

Essential Oils: Spearmint, Peppermint, Rosewood, Basil, Bergamot, Chamomile, Clary Sage, Geranium, Eucalyptus, Geranium, Thyme, Sandalwood

Meditation

Find a comfortable seat or position and close your eyes. Take one deep inhale through your nose, and then open your mouth and release a sigh on the exhale. Do this up to three times. Close your mouth and return to normal breathing. Bring your focus to the tip of your nose, gently inhaling and exhaling. For each breath imagine walking toward a small, climbable mountain. Focus only on your breath and the vision of the mountain as you walk. As you approach the mountain, see yourself climbing effortlessly to the top. Inhale and exhale. Everywhere you look you see beauty and nature, and the vastness of the sky. On your next inhale, imagine spreading your arms wide and slightly tilting your head back, heart and throat shining upward toward the sky. Use this opportunity to declare your truth. On your next exhale, imagine opening your mouth, and at the top of your lungs you will yell out a personal truth. "I want to move!" "I want to be free!" "I'm in love!" "I'm the one who stole the $10!" Whatever you feel inclined to tell the world within the safety of this sacred space, let it roar. You can twirl around, cry, stomp, and dance as you yell. But speak the truth and set it free.

PART III
Transform

CHAPTER 6

Mystic

Mindfulness is about love and loving life.
When you cultivate this love, it gives you
clarity and compassion for life, and your
actions happen in accordance with that.
—Jon Kabat-Zinn

O ur brains are fascinating machines. The brain controls the physical body without command and serves as a warehouse and retrieval system for the functioning of the mind. The brain and mind are distinctly different. The mind controls your energy body and the response to your emotions. Your mind also tries to control your actions and response to the world. It's your choice to be guided by your Soul or by the worry and fear of your mind.

Mindless thought triggers self-deception. Mindfulness triggers conscious thought. Conscious thought should not be confused with positive thought. The goal is not to avoid the negative in life, but to stay connected to our inner selves while responding to the world with compassion and positive input.

There is an ideology that believes every thought manifests our reality. My philosophy is that our thoughts are part of reality and are connected to the universal energy of all thought. Oneness with the Universe is the dynamic that allows us to be empathetic and tap into the consciousness of higher thinking. By doing so, we can affect change in the world. If all things are connected, then all thoughts and emotions are also connected. If we fear and negate parts of our thoughts, we fear and negate part of our reality. This creates more false illusions in the mind. Belief that one thought creates all reality is akin to believing one letter creates a word. We don't build an intelligent vocabulary with just the letter "A." We need all the letters in various combinations to create a rich vocabulary. The same is true with thoughts and emotions. We need all thought and emotion to become more conscious and to create the life that we desire. To deny thought or words is to deny the connection to self and the Universe.

Thoughts are powerful. What we dwell on uses a greater amount of our energy than what we do not dwell on. So, it is important to master the activity of the mind, but not to negate thoughts. You do not want to dwell on one thought entirely, be it negative or positive. We need a variety of thoughts and to be present with those thoughts to live a rich and meaningful life.

Mindfulness

Mindfulness can change your life by expanding your awareness, softening your judgments, and helping you become a better partner. Mindfulness means becoming more aware and focused on the present moment. It is the practice of deep awareness of self and others. This can allow you to slow down, find peace, and deal with the reality of what is in front of you. Being mindful is about being present. The illusion in the minds of many people is that there is a better place, other than the here and now. The illusion is that life is not as we currently see it, but how it will be at a different time. These false ideas keep us trapped as victims to the reality of the mind. If we stay present in the now there's no anxiety or focus on the future because it doesn't exist.

What is often overlooked is that mindfulness does not happen only in the mind. When we follow our inner wisdom, we check into a new dimension of existence that is more in tune with the world. From this place, we use our bodies, our emotions, our five senses, and our mind to fully engage with the present moment. We are astutely aware of the nature of things. We heighten our intuitive powers by becoming mindful in body, emotion, and spirit to the point that the mind serves as a filter that translates our visceral experiences.

Mindfulness is a vibrant aliveness that sets us on the spiritual path. Tuning in with full connection and utilizing all our internal resources is the path toward a most sublime and blissful inner peace.

As you practice mindfulness and conscious thinking, your negative thoughts will serve as messengers. The messages call for you to pay attention to internal needs or needs of the world. For example, constant worry may be a manifestation of a fear-based life (Root Chakra, Chapter 1), a lack of control (Solar Plexus imbalance, Chapter 3), or perhaps a misguided mind in need of meditation or mindfulness practices in this chapter. Negative thinking about

> We are what our thoughts have made us; so take care about what you think. Words are secondary. Thoughts live; they travel far.
> —Swami Vivekannanda

your job may indicate an imbalance in your passion and creativity center (Sacral Chakra, Chapter 2) or you may not be following your core beliefs due to past shame (Solar Plexus Chakra, Chapter 3). Attempting to "turn off" or "let go" of negative thinking about your problems will only distance you from the messages they are trying to deliver. It will also separate you from self-love and inner peace. We need the polarity of thought to experience the reality of our wellness. As you become whole and balanced on your path to healing, your thoughts will naturally gravitate toward those that are more aligned with your heart and Soul, resulting in a natural reduction of habitual of negative thinking.

Fear dwells in the mind but uproots our connection to self and safety. Fear is not who we are and should not control us. The scripture of Timothy that appears on this page was one I memorized during the height of my anxiety. It's a reminder that you were not made to be weak or fearful, but your true nature is that of strength, love, and a useful mind. You can claim that for yourself.

There is rational and irrational fear. Rational fear alerts us to potential danger. Irrational fear originates from false thinking about the unknown. We feel the physical symptoms of fear due to stress hormones released by the endocrine system, which is controlled by the brain. The physical reactions make us even more afraid, as if the fear will take control of our bodies. Unless you are in a stressful situation that warrants fearing for your life, what you experience as fear is typically a ghost that has been created in your mind.

> For He hath not given us the spirit of fear, but of power and of love and of a sound mind.
> —2 Timothy 1:7, The Bible, King James Version

We place so much belief in the power of the mind and it's functioning that we begin to believe the mind is who we are. Are we just the thoughts of our mental reality? If you have no control over your mind, the answer is yes. You must learn how to use the mind in a conscious way and not let it control your behavior. When the mind is unleashed or unguided, it can catch us in its web of illusion.

A fully conscious existence is not possible without our minds, but we must be careful to not allow the mind to play tricks on us. It is like a great magician, creating illusions before our eyes. If we are slaves to our mind, we will interpret life from a limited capacity. Our perception becomes narrowed, our ideas become small, and our beliefs will dwindle. Faith, love, and emotion are not cultivated in thought, they are only judged there.

When your mind controls your experiences, you become like a dog chasing its tail. There is little peace or understanding of emotional or spiritual processes when using the mind alone. We can only spin a thought around so many times before we get a headache or mental fatigue. This is often referred to as monkey mind because, like a monkey, your thoughts will jump and scratch and childishly sidetrack you with worry, chatter, and nonsensical thinking. Your mind is to be used for rational decision-making, focus, and discernment. When it comes to guided wisdom, we need a new understanding of the mind's capacity. Our inner wisdom or intuition is a deeper lens from which we can view the world that leads us to connect to a more meaningful existence.

Creating your reality is a powerful step toward awakening. Accessing your inner wisdom allows the utilization of its many functions of higher consciousness, intuition, greater imagination, and higher perception. Full connection to your heart and mind allows better understanding of the desire and wishes of your Soul and the life you are meant to actualize.

The Brow Chakra

The area of the energy system that governs the brain and mind is the 6th or Brow Chakra, also known as the Third Eye. Many of the physical functions of the eyes, ears, nose, the endocrine system, and the pineal and pituitary glands are in its region. We use this energy center to access our inner wisdom, or intuition, as well as to communicate with our higher power and spiritual Source. The challenge to a healthy and balanced Brow

Chakra is to separate the false illusions of the mind and the essence of who we are. We are not our mind; we are our Soul. It is by believing the illusions of the mind that we block our health due to anxiety and fear. The physical symptoms of an imbalance are:

Hormone imbalances	Brain tumors
Headaches	Sinusitis
Nervous disorders	Eye problems
Insomnia	Hearing issues
High blood pressure	Stroke

Emotional and behavioral imbalances may arise due to following untrue beliefs or ideas while not practicing mindful conscious living. With an imbalanced Brow Chakra, you may experience the following issues.

Rigid thinking	Fear of the unknown
Paranoia	Indecision
Anxiety	Inability to discern information from knowledge
Depression	
Nightmares	Loss of life direction
Prejudice	

Anxiety and the Mind

Behind afflictions such as anxiety, OCD, or phobias are unresolved emotions needing attention. Fear and anxiety run rampant in our society, but there is not much focus on how to address the underlying issues that are creating these issues, only how to mask the problem. The key is to treat the issue rather than the symptom.

If you carry years of repressed shame, OCD may present in your mind as a response to the denied feelings. Anxiety may be the expression of an unresolved heartache or self-worth issues. The external manifestation of repressed emotions trick us into believing we have a condition like anxiety. The presenting symptom, such as anxiety or depression, keeps us from facing the real issue of shame or self-loathing.

Anxiety is a product of stress in the mind, which then causes physical responses. Anxiety may be caused by constant worry, fixating on the future (the unknown), reactions to food intolerances, sensitivities to drugs or alcohol, over-thinking, fatigue, and lack of control over your thoughts. It is often caused by unprocessed emotions such as feeling like you don't belong, feeling angry at your position in life, instability, self-worth issues, lack of direction, shame, and a host of others.

Anxiety, on its own, is not a disease. It is the presentation of a deeper emotional or mental imbalance. It's commonly believed that anxiety is genetic and runs in families. However, much of that can be attributed to learned behavior from family members, feeling the need to empathize and wanting to fit in, relational dynamics, and conditioning. You may believe that fear causes anxiety, which it can if the fear is based in false illusions of the mind and not valid fears of danger. When we experience true fear, there is often no time for anxiety. If we experience memories of the fear, anxiety becomes a symptom of unresolved feelings of fear, and one should focus on feeling grounded and safe. Anxiety is often experienced when you don't allow the time to process the root of your fear and allow healing. You do not have to suffer from anxiety forever.

To live free of anxiety is to allow your fears and accept your feelings. The more you resist anxiety, the more alive it will feel. Nothing is wrong with you except the power you give to the fears in your mind. It's the same with thoughts. Do not run from your thoughts, as it only empowers them to chase you.

Behind every affliction is an unresolved emotion.

Notice what your thoughts are saying and allow them to pass. The fixation on worry and other life issues keeps the mind over-active and in too much control. As the mind becomes tired and weary from overuse, it weakens your system, creating a platform to experience more anxiety.

Recently I was lying down and that familiar sensation of anxiety came over me. It caught me off guard because I hadn't experienced anxiety for a long time and I wasn't aware of any stress. I remained still and breathed into it. I allowed the sensation and acknowledged it with the words "I feel anxious." Within moments of being present with it, a thought of my grandmother who died a few years ago came to mind. I wanted to cry. I realized I had residual grief. I hadn't taken the time to fully process her death and I had pushed aside the sadness of missing her. Finally, I allowed myself to cry and grieve the loss. It was then that the anxiety disappeared.

The next time you experience anxiety, fear, depression, or other negative emotion, take a moment to reflect on what you feel beyond the symptom that is presenting itself. Name the emotion, allow it to speak to you and listen. The more aware you are, the more compassion and attention you can give to your healing. *Warning!* Healing can be scary. You may experience fear during your healing process because as we heal we agree to lose the armor that we've created to shield us from our true feelings. We fear love because we don't want to experience heartache and grief. See if you can find the courage to remain present to your feelings. Emotional healing allows us to understand the balance of all aspects of our nature, not for purpose of control, but to better utilize the elements to work toward harmony and wholeness.

There's another aspect of anxiety that often goes unspoken. Anxiety shackles us to a limited life. Not just in action, but in thought. When we are trapped by anxiety we do not use the power of our minds at our greatest potential. Expanding possibilities of reality comes by awakening our hearts and unleashing the grip of fear in our minds. When we escape the tunnel vision of anxiety, we can see more, do more, contribute more, and evolve. Accessing the fullness of our minds, without the interference of anxiety or fear, allows creative energies to spur us forward, which increases our potential. It is for this reason that we do not define ourselves by our anxiety or any other limitation. If you have anxiety in the moment, then you are having anxiety. If you use the term "I have anxiety" as a general statement about your health, then you are limiting your mind's potential.

The more you believe you "have" a certain disorder or illness, the more it "has" you. We find comfort in labels and organization of thought, but you should not allow negative conditions to exert power over your life. My personal experience indicates that anxiety can be controlled. I suffered extreme anxiety for years and grew up in a family of anxious people, yet I successfully conquered anxiety and it no longer controls my life. This doesn't mean I am anxiety-free. When I am in a fearful situation, I feel anxiety like everyone else. Anxiety and fear are meant to provide messages of potential danger and harm.

Breath and Healing

It is important to clarify the use of breath to address emotional and physical issues. You can use your breath to lower stress, blood pressure, and other symptoms of anxiety or imbalances in the body. Breathing techniques alone should not be considered medicine to cure the underlying issue. However, breath can bring an almost immediate reduction to an anxious state or panic. A deep, full breath has a soothing effect on the body and mind, which allows for a healthier internal response to stress.

There are many helpful tools to relieve anxiety, but remember these aids do not attend to the underlying issue. For example, we know deep breathing calms the body. Breath exercises are helpful in regulating the nervous system and reducing the effects of stress and tension that cause our mind and bodies to constrict. But if your anxiety is due to years of repressed anger, breathing does not address the anger issue. You can breathe through anger to reduce your likelihood of throwing a TV through the window in rage, but breathing doesn't get to the core of your anger. The breath gets you through the byproduct of anger (reactions such as the manufactured emotions of anxiety, rage, or a nervous disorder). These are results of repressed emotions such as anger, fear, or shame. Breathing exercises can help. But anger and other authentic emotions need a different strategy. Think about the cause of your anger and how you are processing it. Anger is the real culprit. Don't apologize for it or be afraid of it, work with it.

The only apology an emotion requires is if the display of an emotion like anger is a result of another emotion that you have not attended to. For example, getting angry with your spouse over leaving the toilet lid up when you are actually harboring hurt feelings because he didn't apologize for missing your birthday is misdirected anger and the genuine hurt feelings must be addressed in order to heal.

Own the anger, accept it, and process it. When you express and accept, you diminish the heat of the emotion. You feel it for what it is and use words, emotion, thought, and compassion to process. Allow it to be present until the anger has transformed into another emotion. The true

Emotional Workout

Take a Moment: It only takes a moment to take a moment. Take a moment to be with yourself. Discover the emotions that are at the root of your suffering. You may experience an immediate shift in your consciousness. To heal is to get in touch with your honest emotions. Being in the present is what allows the emotion to come alive. It's much easier to have an open heart and process emotions when you are grounded and present, feeling safely rooted in your life (Chapter 1). Allow yourself to just be. Express the underlying emotion that bothers you. Cry if you feel sad. Scream your anger into a pillow. Write in your journal if you feel lonely. Once you resolve the underlying emotions, you are on the path to healing.

danger and harm are done by numbing our senses with drugs or distractions. We do this to escape from negative feelings, which leaves us disconnected from the root of our problem, to which we need access so that we can experience the healing we desire.

I encourage and recommend breath-work for a lot of the Emotional Workouts because it helps to focus and center the mind and body. But you should not expect these techniques alone to determine your state of emotional or mental health. They are tools for you to use to affect the symptom of a condition that needs attention.

Distractions

I am the queen of distractions. I have many interests and a mind full of ideas. I can distract myself for days to avoid the task at hand. Writing this book has resulted in a clean house, a detailed car, re-organization of my business, and the launch of a new product line. Who said distractions were a negative thing?

Distractions are big obstacles to the difficult or tedious work in our spiritual or emotional life. The more you are distracted the harder it becomes to tune into your inner guide. We find a multitude of things to fill our time instead of using the time for self-care such as prayer or meditation, relationships, or being present with yourself. Distractions keep us from listening to our dreams, our wisdom, and from experiencing the now.

The more we hide behind distractions the more we disconnect from reality. It's like driving down the road and not knowing how you got there. Your mind is somewhere else and your brain and body are on autopilot. This happens in relationships and in our personal lives as well. One day we may place our priority on personal growth and self-love, but the next day we're headed back to work and lose track of the bigger picture. We don't pay attention to what is happening, how we feel, or the vision of our Souls. Distractions separate us from ourselves.

If you find yourself needing distractions while at your job or that you disengage from your work colleagues, it may be a sign that you need another job situation. We create distractions inside relationships that keep us from communicating and expressing our true feelings in an attempt to hide or cover an issue. Our children, careers, and other family members can become distractions from the attention needed in our personal relationships.

Your cell phone, your family, cleaning, watching TV, and shopping for shoes have a place in life, but they shouldn't replace the time for self-care and emotional wellness.

Intuition

Intuition is a wired system of information that is communicated from your Soul to your heart and then translated by your inner guide, sometimes referred to as your sixth sense or third eye. You know you are following your intuition by physical signs and awareness. As divine knowledge radiates through your body you may experience intuition as physical sensations such as goosebumps, butterflies in the stomach, or Aha! moments of deep knowing. As this lightning-fast information is communicated, your heart accepts the wisdom as true and acts from a place of trust. Problems can arise if the mind intervenes and fear blocks the ability for you to see clearly and take action.

Tapping into this knowledge and using it in your daily life for a Soulful journey and emotional healing requires a holistic approach of listening to the mind, body, and spirit.

Children are intuitive by nature. They have few filters to screen their environment, which explains why they typically believe what they hear and see during their developmental years. If this behavior of trust is encouraged it can lead to a more connected and fulfilling life as they grow up. I remember when I first started to "know" things. I was about 6 years old, however, I lacked the vocabulary to describe what seemed real to me but inexplicable in nature. I saw things that others didn't seem to see. My feelings were beyond the level of sensitive, and I communicated with angels and energies from the other side. Things made sense to me in a way I could not explain, so I kept it private at the time, but it has remained a personal interest to this day. Sometimes the enormity of the energy and emotion scared me, but the connection to this depth of perception has helped me understand the world in a unique way.

These early experiences helped form my current work and spiritual path. I'm amazed how our lives offer connections with no bounds and how we can create completely different experiences with a plethora of choices in our mind, in our hearts, and in our energy. Listening to my intuition, combined with the experiences and traumas I've faced, have made me an intuitive, transpersonal healer with skills to help guide others through their personal Soul transformation. There's nothing mystical about intuition once you trust it as part of yourself. Accessing your intuition isn't a cult activity; it doesn't require a guru and you don't need to ascribe to certain philosophies to tune in to your inner wisdom. You can connect by becoming open, listening to the callings of your Soul, and utilizing the information available to you. You have the inner wisdom needed to guide you to peace and happiness. It's a gift that costs nothing except a little time to practice and trust in the process.

Live Between the Lines

Intuition is like an internal steering wheel. Your heart gives you the destination; your intuition takes you there. It's difficult to trust intuition. Our rational minds want tactile evidence or scientific verification that we can believe what we see. However, intuition is more of a feeling than a thought and it is only confirmed by acting (or not) on the feeling. The hard part about intuition is that you must follow the inner guide before you know if you are on the right track. Although it may seem like an unusual approach, you'll find it's the best way to develop self-trust and self-love.

I call intuition "Living Between the Lines." For example, information is found on the lines of a page. Words are easy to understand and they string together to document a thought. But the intangible is so elusive it can slip by like air between an iron gate—you never knew it was there. Intuition is the same.

The feeling of being "stuck in our head" is common, especially as it relates to business decisions, physical security, or practical life. We make millions of decisions each day and we can become overwhelmed by the pressure to perform, earn and excel, and provide food, shelter, health insurance, or other family needs. We believe our mind knows best in all instances, so we work it to death in an attempt to make good decisions.

The answers, however, often lie in the space between the lines. This can be true even for answers to big decisions. What does this mean exactly? Imagine writing your thoughts on a lined sheet of paper. Can you use your inner wisdom to look between the lines? It's not about what you do or don't say; it's what you feel. Feelings don't necessarily appear on the paper, but this is where the heart-inspired Soulful voice of intuition is found—between the lines of the mind.

Intuition is a very powerful thing, more powerful than intellect.
—Steve Jobs

Clark worked for a company for several years. He eventually received a promotion with a generous raise. Clark felt like he was finally being paid and acknowledged for his value and, even better, the promotion package would allow him full health benefits for his family. Though the promotion was great, it didn't place him in the position he had aspired to within the company, a dream he had worked toward since completing his college degree. After doing his best and taking less-than-ideal pay for 15 years, Clark continued to feel resentful. He justified his feelings by telling himself he would find a way to use his creative energies other ways, like in a hobby. But with family responsibilities, there was little time for fun activities.

Later that month, Clark was offered a job with a different company but it would mean moving his family across the country. The job was similar, but it utilized his talents and creativity in a better way. Additionally, it was a high-level position, allowing him to make a creative impact on his future and that of the company. It was essentially the job he dreamt about. The conflict was the salary level. It wasn't nearly as handsome as his current job and some of the benefits were not included. But the job and its location were superb and the prospects were exciting. Clark had a big decision to make.

Clark spoke to several people about the opportunities at hand, and then considered the pros and cons of each. He created lists and calculated potential living expenses. He researched the cost of living and the quality of schools in the potential new location as well as the housing market. Insurance details, the input from his wife, the age of his parents, the likelihood of job security, and many other factors ran through his mind. Granted, this was a good problem to have, but for Clark, it was one of the "big decisions" of his life.

This is where many of us lose our way. We develop more faith in the "norm" or the safe zone of familiarity than we do in our inner guide. No matter how much he mulls it over, stresses, or worries, no matter what it all looks like on paper, Clark's answer lies between the lines. His Soul journey is calling him to decide with his heart and his inner wisdom. He would love the chance to be more creative and he was honored the employer reached out to seek his talent. He felt like his hard work had paid off and he would realize his dreams. Clark wanted to accept the new job, even if it didn't "stack up" to practicality. His spirit was calling him to go. This is Soulful living guided by his inner voice.

What is your spirit saying to you? Where does your inner voice tell you to go? This is your intuition speaking to you. It's the call to emotional healing, the guidance that has the potential to lead you to transformation.

Intuition can come as flashes of insight that may provide an entirely new direction for your life, or it can be continual communication with yourself—like a good friend helping to steer the way.

In practicing intuition, you will notice that it's often the smaller, day-to-day decisions that hold the true meaning in our lives. These small decisions lead to the "big" ones, and this becomes the framework for your Soul-inspired life. These are seemingly meaningless choices that our intuition provides on a subconscious level without us realizing it. It's important to be awake and aware enough to know the difference between intuition, thought, emotion, and mindfulness.

The difference between the terms *mind* and *intuition* can be confusing because we think of the two as related. But there is a difference. Some people speak of their inner wisdom in terms of rational thought, like they "just knew" it was the right decision. That gut instinct of "just knowing" is your intuition, which is not related to traditional thinking or knowledge. If you experience sleepless nights, headaches, anxiety, or general monkey mind that won't shut off, this is not intuition but your mind in over-drive. The mind is signaling that something is out of balance. If you are often overcome with anxiety, worry, fear, or indecisiveness, you may be giving the mind too much control. You should refocus your thoughts on mindfulness. Rather than rely too much on the mind to make decisions, allow your heart and spirit to participate and lead.

Rational thinking requires the use of the mind for certain tasks, but do not over-use the mind to guide the flow of your life. You have a powerful inner wisdom that is connected to your Soul. Using your inner guide alleviates fear, indecisiveness, and lack of direction. If Clark based his decision on salary alone, that would be a rational decision of the mind. Instead, he chose to follow his heart and intuition.

Spiritual Mapping, which we will practice again at the end of the chapter, can also be a practical tool to help develop and trust your intuition as well as hone the skills of deep listening. Listening to your Soul requires connection to your spiritual source, be it God, angels, spirit guides, ancestors, or whomever you connect to spiritually. Prayer and meditation can be effective ways to get into the practice of listening, if you learn to quiet your mind and body and allow yourself to hear.

Intuitive listening may offer such clarity that you don't realize intuition is speaking. Words or thoughts can filter in and seem like regular ideas. Pay attention to what comes to you, even if it seems out of the norm. A face, name, color, or smell may suddenly come to the forefront. A memory or feeling may appear out of nowhere. These seemingly regular thoughts and ideas could be insights to information you seek. Journaling can help if you have trouble listening.

Emotional Workout

Journaling: Writing is a good practice for intuitive listening. A previous Emotional Workout included free-form writing to remove mental chatter and thought. Journal writing is more focused. Every day, try to spend five to 15 minutes writing in a dedicated journal. Allow yourself to express creatively, with stories or dreams, writing as naturally and unfiltered as possible. Think of it as your adult diary, without overloading it with the latest drama. Express yourself and use your imagination. Doodle. See what inspires you on each day and write about that. You could pick a color or food, an element of nature, or an emotion to write about your thoughts and feelings. Journaling is a wonderful connector of creative energy of the 2nd Chakra and a way to stir the imagination of the 6th Chakra.

Easter Egg Story

On one Easter Sunday morning, I decided to take a long nature walk and then go home to write and reflect. In the afternoon, I sat down to write about intuition. Although it had been a lovely day, I couldn't write. I felt blocked. Self-doubt began to nag at me, and fatigue set in. I closed my eyes and took a nap. Not willingly, because a lot of self-judgment started welling up such as "I'm not doing enough," "I'm not good enough, creative enough. . . ." I checked out for a few minutes and slept.

My grandmother loved church and Christian holidays, so it was natural that I thought of her that day. I missed her. I always hoped to have some mystical connections with my grandma after she passed, but she had not contacted me since she died. No birds, sunsets, messages, or dreams. I thought of her regularly and felt her love, but I wanted something visible. I wanted a sign.

My cat, Cosmo, woke me from the nap, wanting to play. He pranced around a special table in my room where I display several fragile and cherished items. Many of the items were given to me by my grandma. I told Cosmo to get down but he didn't listen. Instead, he went straight for a wooden egg that was nestled among the little statues on the table. He was completely focused on the egg and did everything possible to get the egg off the table. He finally succeeded. I wrangled the egg from his mouth and as I did so, my mind was filled with love for Grandma.

When she passed, I inherited a lovely mink jacket. The wooden egg was in one of the pockets. Grandma never mentioned the egg while she was alive but the egg was something tangible that made me feel connected to her. Since finding it, I have always carried it or laid it on my special table. It was strange that Cosmo, for the first time and on Easter day, was determined to snatch the egg from the table. My grandmother was surely having a fit. She couldn't stand cats!

Later that day I had an appointment with a client at Modern Sage. Although my business is usually closed on Easter, I decided to help a client in need. My intuition told me I should arrive early in case there were customers prior to my appointment. Sure enough, three customers came in as soon as I arrived and one asked for help with anxiety. I was glad I was there.

As I assisted the customers, I noticed something very bizarre. A large crystal egg was misplaced. Instead of it being in a display on the wall where it was the day before, it was on a table in the front of the store. Somehow it had fallen out of the window display and jumped two feet across the table and over a foot-long wooden box to land in a tray of amethyst cross pendants. The egg was the only item that had moved from the window display.

I was amazed that not only had the egg jumped off the wall, it had also found the crosses, and on Easter of all days! Grandma loved God, she loved me, she loved eggs, and she loved crosses. Ironically, when I purchased the variety of gemstone crosses to sell at Modern Sage, I thought she would have liked the jade one, but she picked amethyst.

I'm convinced that Grandma was not only with me celebrating Easter that day, but she was also reminding me of the miracles of life, the connection of love, and the importance of being present to my inner wisdom.

This was truly a magical Easter day. With mindfulness in my heart and spirit, I watched my intuition unfold. The experience resurrected my desire to write. My connection to Grandma invited me to witness the

> The intuitive mind is a sacred gift and the rational mind is a faithful servant. We have created a society that honors the servant and has forgotten the gift.
> —Albert Einstein

power of spirit at work; to connect to my intuitive self, to help others, and to create. The egg is a wonderful symbol of creation and the experience gave me new ideas for this book.

When you are quiet you can hear your Soul speak to the direction you should take. Whether it feels inspired or not, try to follow it. That's the magic of intuition. If we listen, it's possible to participate in the miracles that constantly unfold around us. Our minds and hearts connect to the body and spirit allowing us to witness the natural and supernatural flow of life. The "signs" are there if we look. None of these events on Easter were in my original plan. I was supposed to stay at a beach house to write that weekend. Because I went with my internal flow it turned out to be a wonderful day.

It isn't feasible or healthy to spend all your time looking for signs, but the joys of the world will unfold when you are connected to your inner resources in appropriate ways. This way of living allows for more trust in the path that is laid out for you.

Whatever your religious beliefs, resurrection is possible for each of us, in every moment. It's the phoenix rising, the spirit that never dies. If you

Emotional Workout

Visualization Practice: Use visualization to awaken your intuition as well as express your creativity. It's like productive daydreaming. Create a goal for next year. With your eyes open or closed, spend five minutes imagining how you will accomplish this goal. Plan the details of how you will achieve it. Visualize the different steps and activities that get you to the goal. Be as specific as possible. If your goal is a trip to Italy, imagine purchasing the tickets. What will you wear on the plane ride? See yourself eating brunch at a café in Rome. What is the weather like? Imagine interacting with locals. This is an effective way to train the mind to live consciously and to enhance the energy of your imagination. It's also fun!

feel blocked, scared, lost, or disconnected, be still and listen to your inner guide. What you hear will be the call of your Soul.

More Than Meditation

The new trend is to spiritually levitate. Many people are trying to solve all their problems with yoga and meditation. Don't get me wrong, I'm a long-time practitioner of both, but we need to remember how to balance and flow. Meditation is an important practice to include in your self-care life, but it shouldn't be the only one. It's like the next fad diet. The big boom in mindfulness has sparked deeper interest in spiritual quests and helped put meditation into the mainstream market. That's good, but relying solely on meditation is like relying on an apple a day to stay healthy. If you continue bad habits, an apple is not going to solve all your health needs, nor should you count on meditation to solve all your emotional or mental needs. However, with the right intentions and a holistic approach to peace and happiness, meditation can make a significant difference.

Meditation is popular because of the positive results people receive from the practice, including better sleep, greater focus, less headaches, a reduction in anxiety, general relaxation, and better job performance. Although meditation offers these benefits, it's important to note that meditation is more than relaxing or quieting the mind.

Meditation is about discovering and connecting to your true self and your deeper nature. As you spend time focused on the present moment, the mind's chatter settles down. Physical distractions and bodily yearnings become less gnawing, allowing you to go deep into your being. The more you access this inner sanctuary, the more you develop trust in yourself and your emotions. Sitting in a quiet refuge and focusing on your thoughts and emotions helps to decrease the intensity of them.

Some people have trouble with meditation because they are trying to turn off their mind. I encourage my clients to think about the roles of parent and child. Children make a lot of noise and movements to get your attention. They cry, scream, dance, and interrupt you a million times a day. The more you ignore or rebuke them, the more they scream and nag. If you sit with the child and give him your full attention, the child becomes satisfied because he feels heard and loved. The screaming stops and the child can go back to being a child, playing and exploring. Thoughts, like children, ask for your attention. Sit with your thoughts like you would sit and listen to a child. Allow the messages your thoughts are trying to send and be present. When that thought leaves, you can welcome the next thought. You are not trying to shut off the mind, because the mind is there to think; that is its job. As you become the parent to your mind, you can begin to control the pace and activity of the mind, and learn to decipher fear from truth.

This simple method is calming and soothing for the mind. For at least five minutes a day, sit down, be quiet and be still. Be mindful to not use your meditation practice as an escape or method of control. Meditation is positive, but I see people become imbalanced on their quest to achieve an experience other than what they have now. Becoming fixated on reaching new spiritual levels may cause the loss of reality in the real world. We need to maintain equal focus on staying present, on intimacy, on creativity, and opening our hearts.

The power of meditation can transform lives, but it's not to be used to somehow make us seem better or more spiritual than others, or our previous self. Becoming judgmental is not the goal. To focus all your energy on the mind or on achieving higher consciousness can create dysfunction. In my work, I've seen too many people separate from the experiences of the world and their emotions in the quest for spiritual enlightenment. Examples of this behavior include flightiness, disorganization, the inability to connect with others, or becoming fearful of normal experiences. Meditation is not about results-oriented thinking or actions.

A young woman came to me for help with her 6th Chakra. She was studying meditation in her spiritual life with prayer and inner work, but she felt blocked. She told me she meditated several times a day and used crystals and oils. I could tell she was frustrated because she wasn't having the results she wanted after such an intense practice. She wanted freedom from worry and the world, but instead she was more worried than ever. As I read her energy and chakras I noticed an imbalance, but it wasn't in her mind. The imbalance was in her Root and Sacral Chakras and it was very physical in nature. She had a severe lack of nutrients and a systemic yeast infection. Her entire body and energy system were working overtime to deal with the negative reactions to certain foods. Most of her energy was used to restore physical balance. She struggled to focus and meditate because she was suffering and she had lost sight of her physical health. It's

Emotional Workout

Aromatherapy: Natural essential oils are derived from plants and they have been used medicinally for centuries. They have a healing effect on our emotions, bodies, and minds. For anxiety, depression, or to improve concentration, I recommend applying essential oils around the head region or using them in a nebulizing diffuser. If applying directly to the skin, use a carrier oil such as grapeseed, almond, or coconut oil. Add approximately one drop of your favorite essential oil for every three drops of carrier oil and blend. Apply to your temples, at the base of your neck, or directly to your Brow Chakra. (Modern Sage has a blend called Mystic that is formulated to help open this chakra.) For use on the body or in a diffuser, choose oils that brighten or awaken your senses such as Rosemary, Geranium, or Clary Sage. Lavender, Bergamot, or Neroli help to calm and restore. Spiritual oils such as Frankincense, Myrrh, and Sandalwood are helpful for prayer or meditation practice.

not possible to exist in the cosmos full-time without real-world ramifica-tions. I helped her get back to health and restoration by suggesting a new diet plan, including more protein and probiotics as well as removing food allergens. We also increased her exercise program and feelings of connec-tion to the earth. She now feels much healthier and stable. She's found a balance in the responsibilities of being human while simultaneously seek-ing higher consciousness.

Brow Chakra Basics

Colors: Indigo

Gemstones: Amethyst, Angelite, Fluorite, Azurite

Essential Oils: Thyme, Holy Basil, Rosemary, Clary Sage, Lavender, Neroli, Cypress, Jasmine, Orange, Chamomile, Myrrh, Juniper, Berry

Meditation

With comfortable shoes and clothing for outdoor walking, allow 10 to 20 minutes for walking meditation. Walk barefoot if possible. Walk with intention and ease, rather than trying to achieve great distance or speed. Start by focusing on the bottom of your feet. Be sure the bottom of your feet touch the ground fully with each step. For several breaths, allow your mind to focus only on your movement. Watch your feet but look ahead and walk with comfort. As you continue walking, notice what is in front of you and look at it with full awareness. If there is a tree, consider the tree. Be aware of its colors, size, and shape. Perhaps you see a car or a person. Give it the same slow, mindful attention. During the meditation walk, allow yourself to go where your feet lead. You may use the mantra with your breath, "I am divinely guided." Repeat the mantra as you step and allow your mind and body to relax.

Spiritual Mapping

Use a blank sheet of paper and a pen or pencil. This map will be a tool to develop and practice your intuition skills.

Create a mark in the center of your page and name it Heart. Next, think of a decision you need to make or event that is coming up within a three- to six-month period. You may be considering a move, a new job, a change of relationship, or adopting puppies. Pick just one. On the right-hand corner of the page, place a mark and write the name of the decision that needs to be made. Between your heart center and the decision, place five marks, evenly spaced.

The purpose is to work your way from the heart center to the event using intuitive listening. In the previous map (Chapter 4) you worked from the event to the heart center. In this exercise, work from the heart to the decision.

Take a moment to become centered and breathe. Relax your brow and do a quick body scan. Be aware of how you feel and try to find a state of relaxation and open energy flow. Try not to work with intuition when you're exhausted, angry, or feeling emotional fragile. If you feel lazy, find another time to create your map. Laziness leads to guessing.

When you are fully present with the decision in your mind and trust in your heart, use these questions to guide you: 1) Is this something I want? 2) How does it feel in my body? 3) If there were no other considerations, what does my heart advise me to do? 4) Is this good for me and why? 5) What is the right direction for me right now? Answer these questions next to the five marks.

Use your first instinct and write your feelings next to the mark. In the silence of your heart and Soul, see what is revealed. No matter what you hear, write it down. It could be a clue or description of what this event may look like when it happens. If you see green, write green. That may signify the color of the door on your new home. When you finish, put the map in a safe place and revisit it at the time of your decision. Intuition is a beautiful practice of mindfulness. To see if you're on track you must pay close attention to your inner voice and be externally aware. You are brave to delve deeper into the Soul and trust your own guidance. Good job!

CHAPTER 7

Ascend

Every moment and every event of every man's
life on Earth plants something in his soul.
—Thomas Merton

This book highlights the impact that fear, guilt, shame, and grief has on humans and how to process and heal the pain. We seek happiness and peace, and it is only through connection and acceptance that we can reach that goal. Emotional healing requires putting your broken pieces back together again. To mend your heart, you must have access to your suffering. To do this you must be willing to tear down the walls that create the confines of your emotional prison.

Through time we learn to avoid suffering by lying to ourselves and others, which serves to increase emotional distress and disconnection. These are the negative energy patterns we use in attempt to separate from pain. However, it is through connection to our divine nature that we can be free. To be whole and healthy, it is necessary to accept and process the suffering and be open to the guidance and direction of Source, the Creator, the great Conductor. I call this energy "God." As we walk in faith and connection to Source, we find balance between spirit and body, between heaven and earth. A rich spiritual life leads us to a satisfying and peaceful human life. This is the final link to healing. Integrating spiritual wisdom with earthly experience allows us to emotionally process and evolve.

Enlightenment is achieved with the alignment of heart and Soul. Every experience in our lives offers exactly what we need to heal and grow into this alignment. If experiences are dismissed or abandoned, the progress of our spiritual evolution grinds to a halt. Our purpose is to stay connected to all our experiences and emotions so we walk toward the alignment and experience true self-love and peace. Because we are so unique, our paths to healing must be unique. That is why we are each given different experiences to process and endure in our lives. As we process the suffering in our life, our hearts are free to participate in our higher purpose. Emotional healing is important because it is the path that allows you to reach your true purpose.

The more connected to Source, the deeper we can dive into our human experience.

The quest for peace and happiness is fulfilled through the process of emotional healing. If we avoid healing, we become trapped by the illusions of our minds. Our minds trick us to believe that peace and happiness are achievable only if we do something different or better. There is the illusion that earthly attachments will make us feel better with more money, the coolest car, or the new drug. These false beliefs mask the need for healing. It will not suffice to depend on external things to satisfy the internal war of emotional distress. Peace comes from your Soul, not from mental illusions.

Shifting your perspective from how you view the reality of your mind to the reality of your Soul helps define who you are. This is where you heal and gain insight to why bad things happen to good people. It is from the Soul that we can accept our weaknesses and move from fear to greatness. The more we heal, the more access we have to the alignment and reality of our divine being. It is from this place that we can experience the peace and happiness that we crave.

The spiritual path is a difficult one for many. It symbolizes vast ideologies that include acceptance of things such as compassion, love, and grace. It is believed that we must surrender our own desires or needs for that of the larger cosmic plan. The more you commit to healing and aligning your heart with your Soul, the easier it becomes to accept the aspects of spirituality.

It is your responsibility to tap into the connection of your divine presence. It's scary to rely on faith and trust in yourself. It may require that you go against what other people think you should do or who you should be, but it's possible to find happiness on this path.

The Crown Chakra

The 7th, or Crown Chakra, is the last main chakra center recognized as dominant to our general health system. The Crown Chakra is located at the top of the head and radiates upward. Otherwise known as the "Gateway to Spiritual Wisdom," this energy center helps us access our higher selves and divine purpose. It is from this place that we connect to God and the oneness of life. When the Crown Chakra is healthy and in the flow, we feel free, aware, and trusting in the order of life. Many people will experience an expanded perspective and harmony with the universe from this place, and it governs how we respond to the world around us. It is from this energy, connected to the heart and Soul, that we seek peace, nirvana, and enlightenment.

Many people have blocked their spiritual beliefs due to negative memories from their childhood or out of anger toward God. If you were forced to attend church or uphold rituals that you did not agree with, you may have turned away from religion or faith altogether, or perhaps you seek something different to fulfill your own beliefs. The challenge then becomes figuring out what you truly believe. If you blame God for a bad situation, or find it impossible to believe a higher power would allow negative things to happen in the world, you may shut down trust in a spiritual source. It's not uncommon to see the Crown Chakra energy blocked due to resentment, pain, rebellion, or anger. When we block our belief system, we are unable to translate our inner wisdom and life purpose into reasonable life experiences.

There comes a point when we feel weary or unable to handle life on our own. Crossing over the threshold into emotional adulthood is a time of spiritual transformation, but it can be confusing. Those of us that have a faith in a higher power turn to the energy of comfort through prayer or community. Those who have not developed or nurtured a spiritual foundation often have a noticeable imbalance in their lives. The Soul may nudge us to reconnect through the emergence of physical or emotional symptoms. Physical symptoms of a block in the Crown Chakra may present themselves in the following ways:

Migraines	Brain tumor
Neurological disorders	Schizophrenia
Insomnia	Bi-polar disorder
Dyslexia	Depression
Dementia	Nerve pain
Addictions	Multiple sclerosis
Delusions	Parkinson's disease

Emotional imbalances may also arise from blocked energy or disconnection from your higher self.

Lack of direction

Frustration

Stress

Emotional distress

Loneliness

Isolation

Cynicism

Lack of faith

Anger toward God

Fear of death

Indecision

Disorientation

Lack of joy

Unclear life purpose

Apathy

Inability to set or maintain goals

Spiritual distress

Messiah complex

Spiritual Guidance

The more we are guided spiritually, the more wisdom, joy, and peace can be attained. We need the balance and strength that comes from a faith in something beyond the confines of our minds. There is great relief as we tune into our spiritual wisdom and faith, because our minds attempt to make us believe in the false promises of the world. The mind tells us that we will be free of our hardships and turmoil if we work harder or make more money. But it is only through the connection to your divine being that ultimate freedom is possible. As you become emotionally healed you align more closely to your Soul where peace reigns.

> Belief consists in accepting the affirmations of the soul; unbelief, in denying them.
> —Ralph Waldo Emerson

By accepting and trusting that suffering and joys are part of a greater plan for our lives, we connect to our divine selves and loneliness is relieved. This requires welcoming the unknown and working through our fears. On the fearless path, shame softens into love, and guilt becomes compassion. We can walk in faith and know love. Love transcends the belief that the world will provide the relief we seek. Relief is within you, and connected to your Soul.

Your spirit is the expression of your Soul. You are divine energy that is perfectly made with a unique and guided personality and purpose. Your Soul does not change, but your relationship to your Soul may change. Prayer, meditation, and spiritual work are things that connect to your Soul. The nature of prayer and meditation carries a high vibration energy, which is more in tune with the vibration of divine energy. As you become one with your true self and create the openness for the heart to give beyond what is materially possible, you connect with the frequency of divinity.

Emotional Workout

Yoga: Certain yoga poses are very helpful to increase blood flow and energy to the crown of the head. Most inversion postures, where the head is below the heart, are excellent poses. These include headstands, shoulder stands, and forward bends. Unless you are an advanced yogi, start with the forward bend. Place your feet hip distance apart. Slightly bend your knees and slowly fold over. Let your arms hang loose or hold opposite elbows. Release the tension in your neck, allowing your head to hang freely. If this pose bothers your back, bend your knees more. Stay in this pose for five to 10 breaths if possible, then slowly roll up to standing. This exercise is good to do upon rising in the morning or any time you feel stress, mental fog, or disconnected.

Spiritual faith is a belief structure that is unique to you. Beliefs are often based on what we've been told to believe. It's important to discover your own beliefs and ensure they are attuned to your heart.

Be careful not to aim low in your spiritual quest. The mind can limit the possibilities of the world, including the potential of knowledge, our personal lives, love relationships, and spiritual beliefs. Harnessing divine energy makes all things possible, including the extraordinary.

An extraordinary experience in my life happened when I was in a church youth group. We were a small group of teens who traveled and performed concerts at retreats, churches, and communities. On one occasion, we were in Michigan on a mission trip where we performed an outdoor concert in a large neighborhood park. There were a dozen singers and musicians, with the usual speakers, mics, and cords running in all directions.

As we rehearsed, we encountered technical difficulty. The sound wasn't working. The leader searched everywhere for another electrical outlet, but we were outdoors, where the options were limited in the public park. We had passed out flyers all week, so the audience was enthusiastic and growing in number. Time was of the essence to get the sound working or all our efforts would have been in vain. Our leader Tim saw an older house across the street. He attached a long extension cord to make the distance and we hoped the home owners would agree to let us use their electricity. He rang the doorbell but there was no answer. He rang and rang. It was our only hope. The crowd was waiting and of course we teens were chomping at the bit to perform and sing our hearts out for our new friends. After a few minutes, Tim walked around the house and found a door cracked open. He pushed on it and inside by the door was an outlet. He connected to the outlet and ran back to start the concert.

Our performance was well received and we had a great time. There was an undeniable energy in the air and the crowd was thrilled with the show. Lives were changed that night.

After the show, a resident in the neighborhood had noticed our struggle with the sound and asked Tim how he solved the electricity problem. Tim pointed to the house across the street. The local man said that house had been abandoned for years, and there was no way electricity would be coming from it. It was a miracle, as there was no other reasonable explanation for what occurred.

If we allow ourselves to witness the divine order of things, we can see miracles happen every day. They may not be life-saving miracles with neon lights, but the miracles and connection of life become huge in the eyes of a spiritually tuned in person. This is the divinity that connects us to each other.

Peace

We all desire peace, but most people look for it in the wrong place. Peace is not found in your mind. We often think of the saying "peace of mind," but we can't rely on the mind to give us the peace that is desired from our Souls. The mind begs for our attention, but there is no stability or peace if we react to every thought from the mind. We are certainly equipped with the ability to process and have peace, but we must harness and utilize the energy that is available from the Source, which connects us to our being. Everyone has access to this kind of peace.

True peace is possible by connecting to your Soul. Peace is a profound emotion that acts as the stepping stone to enlightenment. Lasting peace does not dwell in the body or mind, or in our hearts. True peace comes from the connection to the Soul and divine energy.

Peace is not passive.

When you are "at peace" you meet the essence of your Soul, the existence that transcends the reality of this world. It's the peace that overrides all emotion. It's an assurance that you can trust in the greater plan, and you can rest in the greater plan, and you can rest in your Soul when times get tough. At peace, we are in a beautiful resting place that reminds us of home.

It's not possible to just decide to be at peace; you must find and nurture it. This kind of peace takes effort. There is nothing passive about peace. It requires practice, awareness, and commitment to shepherd in the experience of real peace. Do not be the sheep, be the shepherd.

Peace is not about seeking, but about doing. Peace comes as a result of staying fully connected to your experiences, your emotions, your Soul. Peace allows you to find space within to negotiate each breath of life and decide what you will do with the energy of that breath. There's nothing lazy about peace. It's hard work. It's a supremely courageous move. You must be brave to say what you feel, stay vulnerable in your heart, and trust in the unknown while carrying your pain along for the ride.

Peace requires that you stay connected to your Soul and divine purpose. It asks you to be accountable for your feelings and not to place blame. Peace relies on a faith in the greater plan and the work of the Creator. We find encouragement in our quest for peace to put compassion, empathy, and forgiveness to work. Peace is our incentive for emotional healing.

Our spirit craves peace. Once you realize that your peace comes from a connection to your Soul, you will not be controlled by your mind. You will experience more and more peace by aligning your heart to your Soul, and you do that by processing emotions.

There is nothing neutral about peace; it's a radical way to live. To seek this way of life is courageous and gives your life a new dimension. It's the energy of confidence, the beauty of strength, and the glow of awakening. Companies

> There is no path to peace. Peace is the path.
> —Gandhi

try to capture the essence of peaceful, Soulful living by using special imagery in their advertising. They know that consumers desire and covet this sublime way of being.

Prayer and Meditation

Your Soul has a voice, an energy, and a commitment to the greater good. Prayer and meditation are the keys to opening and maintaining a healthy relationship to your higher power and to the responsibility of the collective consciousness. When you sit in prayer, reflection, or meditation you become more in tune with the voice of your Soul, to the connection with others and to the Creator.

We pray and meditate to honor and connect with our true nature and to the Creator. It is not an act to judge ourselves or others. I hear people classify others by their spiritual works. They say things like, "She's the best Christian I know" or, "He's so spiritual; he meditates every day"; or people qualify one's good deeds or suggest their way of life as being better or worse than others. There's nothing more antithetical than judging spirituality. Prayer and meditation are very personal and Soulful experiences. Only you know the path to self-love.

There are many things in divine order that we cannot understand or control. Faith in this divine order comes in surrendering to a Higher Power. That doesn't mean we should be passive. To believe in divine order, one must be a participant in life and not just expect "the universe" to hand over our next job, relationship, or financial downfall. While trusting in the divine order, we accept every life experience as it comes, positive or negative. As we do this, we stay connected to something greater than ourselves.

Many people pray or encourage prayer only in times of trial, illness, loss, or other personal crises. This is emergency prayer, and seems to be acceptable in our society, whereas maintenance prayer is not as tolerated in public. We are free people but are encouraged to express our spiritual inclinations primarily in private. Prayer has been taken from schools, the workplace, and from displays on mainstream media. You are more likely to be granted smoke breaks at work rather than meditation breaks. Being strong and focused in our spiritual life requires us to be strong and focused in our beliefs.

People who view life from a mystical perspective often have greater trust in intuition or psychic abilities, and perhaps expect miracles to be part of their daily lives. People who fear these qualities simply fear the connection to their highest nature. Being intuitive and open to your highest spiritual wisdom should not be antithetical to any belief. This misconception is another means to block our connectivity to the divine. This is not to say that we each hold the power of God, but we do have the power to use our senses bestowed on us by the Creator. That includes spiritual wisdom.

> Prayer is not asking. It is a longing of the soul. It is daily admission of one's weakness. It is better in prayer to have a heart without words than words without a heart.
> —Mahatma Gandhi

Emotional Workout

Prayer: Challenge yourself to the humble exercise of prayer. Regardless of your spiritual beliefs, allow yourself to bow down to the greater energy of creation. There's no secret formula to prayer. Just open your heart and share. Open your mind to listen. Speak from the deepest place of your being and trust that you are heard and loved. Sit in quiet contemplation, being aware of your thoughts and feelings, and trust that you are being divinely guided. Try to connect to the shared energy of your higher consciousness and have a dialogue from your heart. What do you need or desire? What is troubling your mind or body? Share this with gratitude and acknowledgement that your needs are being met.

If we fear the gifts of guidance, we have an excuse not to heal our inner turmoil. In other words, we continue blaming the world, or God, or thanking the world, or God, for signs of relief or prosperity or good fortune. We externalize our inner experience into a higher power rather than taking responsibility for the suffering or problems in our lives. For example, if we believe all things happen for a reason, or if we surrender our lives to God's will, we then have a back-up system to excuse the unwanted areas of life. This prohibits us from our work of healing, self-love, and spiritual evolution. There is a divine order to all things, but part of that divine order is providing what you need in order to fully reconnect with your Soul. God's will is not for you to suffer. I believe God's will asks you to process the suffering in a way that leads you closer to your divine nature.

An imbalance in the Crown Chakra is common. When I see this in clients, it's often because they have not maintained or found their beliefs in adulthood. For some, religious beliefs were forced on them as children, only to create resentments or distrust later in life. Some people report that they had negative experiences at church camps or they were embarrassed by their hippie parents chanting in meditation when their school friends came over. Others have never found a belief system at all, living with a vague sense of disconnection to a deep part of their Soul.

It's important to claim and name your spiritual beliefs. Even if they are different than the views of your parents or others it's still possible to connect in your own personal way. Perhaps there's not an official name for what you believe, but you can give it one. If spirituality is absent from your life you will miss the opportunity to have harmony with nature, with others, and with your Soul.

Do not minimize the fact that a higher power is connected to all things and it is the energy that gives guidance to your experience. It's increasingly popular to claim a vague spiritual belief. Because of the pain or anger we experienced with religion in our past, many people adopt the general term *Spiritual* as their label. Or they pray to *the Universe*. I invite you to search your heart and be specific, using forgiveness, love, and intuition to declare what your spiritual truths actually are.

I am a Christian Mystic. I find great comfort in spiritual traditions and have blended several traditions to form the foundation of my beliefs. I've walked down the aisle to save my soul more times than I can count. The symbolism and ritual of baptism was a significant part of my life. The significance of grace and the power of resurrection resonates in my heart. It assures me that I can rise from my ashes and I will be loved forever.

I practice other spiritual traditions as well. The ancient rituals of Native Americans and Shamanic healing ceremonies such as sweat lodges and smudging help ground and connect me to the Earth. I incorporate these practices into my life and work daily. Hindu traditions such as yoga, meditation, and chanting make a deep connection to my energy system, the breath of life, and the health of my body. I utilize this foundation of the energy system and wellness as a baseline in my work. Chinese medicine and Taoist philosophy provide concepts of health for daily life and the recovery of body and mind. I read spiritual texts from mystics and philosophers from around the world. I believe there is one Source, yet various ways to call upon this higher energy to guide us. It's important to find a belief structure that works for you. That part of your life balances the health and energy system of your whole.

Awakening and Enlightenment

Spiritual awakening and enlightenment are goals for many. We are taught that if we free our mind, loose our attachments, and let go of all grief, fear, and anger we'll be in position to attain enlightenment. But enlightenment is not subject to rules and regulations. True enlightenment comes by living in alignment with our Soul. Achieving self-love is possible when you live from your true nature and stay open to emotional processing. The energy of love allows us to experience happiness, intuition, forgiveness, compassion, and peace.

It is not possible to attain a flawless character. Nor can the mind be void of mental activity for more than flashes in time. We will never spontaneously combust into a God-like being, able to live without the necessities of life. But we can live a life that is divinely guided and inspired by our inner wisdom, which leads to awakening and self-love.

Recently I was asked to conduct chakra readings for a community event held at a local bar. Being a healer at a bar proved to be quite popular! A woman named Sue told me of her severe career stress. Using my hands and a pendulum, I did a quick reading on her and found that her Crown Chakra was blocked, her Brow Chakra was over-active, and her Solar Plexus Chakra was imbalanced. Sue was struggling with self-doubt about a work situation. Her mind was filled with worry and causing her excess stress. When I asked if she used meditation or had a regular spiritual practice she fumbled for an answer. She had been relying on her mental resources alone to control her world. Sue had trouble controlling her thoughts and was not seeking guidance from her higher power.

She feared the new business that she had started might fail. The business venture was something that she always dreamed about, and Sue started with gusto using all her passion and drive to take action. She began her mission following the inspiration of her higher self. Yet, in the reality of her work days, she began to doubt the reality of her dreams and worry took over. She was trying to out-think her problems but nothing was improving. In an effort to avoid failure, she just wanted to give up and quit.

> Enlightenment is
> when a wave realizes
> it is the ocean.
> —Thich Nhat Hanh

When our egos and minds get carried away we begin to believe we can handle anything with thought and concentration, so we stop relying on Source. We forget to listen to our higher self or trust divine guidance. The busier we become, the more prayer and meditation take a back seat to everything else. Relying solely on the mind makes it easier to lose connection with who we really are. When the going gets tough, we then feel lost because we are not plugged in and accessing our true resource. We've disconnected from our Souls and can't hear our deeper wisdom. It's like a broken energy circuit that sputters and spews rather than functioning properly. This disconnection can be an issue in all areas of emotional processing, but it's a particular concern with spirituality.

I encouraged Sue to reconnect with something greater than her own mind like her Source. She began crying in the bar because she knew that she was disconnected and she missed the relationship with a higher power. She compared her lack of spiritual connection to losing a family member. Your Soul communicates with you in ways that is impossible to explain, but it is the most intimate connection you will ever have. This spiritual place is where you begin to relate, trust, rest, and receive guidance. Conscious connection to your higher power is a meditation of the mind and heart. Your Soul guides the experience that is the true path to happiness.

> Spiritual awakening happens when you are ready. Not when the environment is right.

Some people use awakening and enlightenment to judge wisdom and purity. It is an aspiration to be "right" or better and to be somewhere else than where we are. This "rightness" becomes a mission of the ego rather than a natural inclination of the heart. This pursuit is based on judgment and low self-worth. Judgment is based in fear. Separateness is based in fear. Acceptance is based in love. Love liberates. As we mature and evolve we realize that the more we accept our weaknesses, the more we position ourselves for awakening.

There's a prayer I use to remind myself of the value of my imperfections:

Help me avoid perfection. Perfection has no place on my path to happiness.

There is no better or right place to be in our spiritual evolution than where you are right now. There is nothing to judge your worth against; your value stands alone. The quest for perfection is simply an excuse to stay immobilized by fear. We know we cannot achieve perfection, so chasing the dangling carrot occupies our minds and distracts us from our real goal of healing.

People work hard to master these concepts and it is easy to become imbalanced on the quest. The mind tries to control the journey of our Soul. The mind tells us that to self-actualize and have otherworldly experiences of bliss and nirvana, we must put forth an intense effort of goodness and correct action. The mind also tempts us with the possibility of a better life once we experience these altered spiritual states. The truth is that awakening and enlightenment do not arrive with bells and whistles. There are no trumpets or parties to celebrate the big moment. In fact, this personal experience is often not a big moment at all, but a slow and progressive way of living that comes by doing our emotional and spiritual work.

Awakening is a by-product of inner peace and healing. It has nothing to do with your possessions, or lack thereof, or how many hours you meditate. You can't earn your way to awakening or enlightenment. Spiritual awakening comes when you follow the guidance of divine wisdom.

Sitting on a mountain-top in a robe at an ashram in India or going on a voyage to a third-world country does not create enlightenment. Awakening doesn't occur because you give your worldly possessions away. Not only are these maneuvers unnecessary for healing and awakening, the fantasy of acquiring enlightenment by enacting a particular scenario keeps many people from doing the work right here, right now in their life. I've had experiences of transcendence in a beat-up 1992 Isuzu, sitting on a porch in Kentucky, and walking through Times Square during rush hour. Awakenings happen when you are ready, not when the environment is right.

Years after becoming freed of addiction and self-abuse, I experienced my most powerful awakening. I have had glimpses or moments of what felt like true peace and connection to God in the past, but this instance was unique. It was the closest I have come to nirvana.

I was driving down a busy street in a culturally diverse neighborhood. It's a road I travel often. The sidewalks were covered with litter and were lively with people hurrying past local gas stations, tire shops, electronic repair stores, and corner markets. It was an average, urban stretch of the bustling metropolis where I live. And between 5th Street and the corner bodega is where it happened. It was an experience of powerful awakening. My mind was weightless, my heart center exploded open, and it was as if I could feel my Soul lift me to another dimension. I have never felt so blissful, connected, or understanding of the world. For those few minutes, everything in my life experience made complete sense. Life was real. I felt alive, free, and at complete peace. The world was in divine order, and all things were perfect. Life appeared like a 3D movie. It was profound joy and bliss. I had broken through the illusions of the earth and lived for a few minutes in an unknown dimension. It was the happiest point in my life.

I was not trying to achieve anything that day outside of the ordinary, but I had subconsciously prepared for the experience by using healing and self-growth practices for many years. The environment around me had nothing to do with my awakening. The streets were filled with trash and the sky was gray. I was driving an average car on an average weekday in a busy city. But my heart and spirit were ready to connect to my Soul and allow me to view life with a new perspective.

I want to encourage you to not lose sight of the possibilities for life. As you do your inner healing work, you will make great strides toward living a more soulful, connected, and peaceful life. The expression of self-love may even manifest as an enlightening experience. Many of us approach the quest for happiness and peace from the wrong direction. We try to force an experience into our mind and emotions, thereby hoping to affect an overall change and be "more spiritual." You can't make "spiritual." You can become more spiritual only as much as you can become more human. You can, however, connect more fully to your Soul and the spiritual realm.

What do you need to do now, today, to be grounded and accepting, mindful and heart-centered? Now is the best time and place to make awakening and happiness possible.

Emotional Workout

Reiki: Energy work such as Reiki is a wonderful way to keep your energy system and body in balance. Reiki is a Japanese technique for relaxation and restoration that promotes healing. The hands-on technique can balance the chakras by sending loving, healing energy to restore the positive flow throughout your system. It's like a massage for your energy system.

Michael was new in town and came to Modern Sage to inquire about meditation. Within minutes of our meeting he shared his emotional crisis. Michael had been abused his entire life by his father, and later by the woman he recently left. His divorce devastated his spirit, left him for broke, and estranged from his son. In our conversation, I saw the terror and desperation in his eyes. Michael was on the edge. This life experience forced him to face his Soul. Would he wither or blossom?

Michael is a 45-year-old dad with movie-star looks. He works in Manhattan in the technology sector. From the outside, he resembled the other five million hipsters running around the city, but on the inside he was a broken-hearted, fearful boy.

His father was verbally, emotionally, and physically abusive. One of five children, Michael was yelled at, called names like "Pretty Boy," and told he was nothing but a "pain in the ass." His father took Michael and his attractive sister to underground, grimy studios that posed as photography houses in Queens. The children were taken advantage of, with his father's blessing. Michael was forced to keep his dad's secrets.

Most nights, Michael went to bed hungry, as there wasn't enough money to buy food for the family. He would eat out of trash cans when the others were asleep. He found fat and scraps from leftover meats, or he'd collect and congeal juices from pot roasts and eat it to fill his hunger before bed. As he grew older, his confusion grew as he learned of his father' expensive hobbies, including high-end photography, model airplanes, and custom cars built from scratch in the garage.

Although Michael and his siblings were hungry, he was starving in other ways that had nothing to do with food. Michael was never nurtured, nor was he allowed to explore life or follow his dreams. He was not even allowed to travel outside the state of New York.

In older years, Michael became resentful of his father's behavior and abuse. However, Michael's shame led him to believe that he deserved the abuse and he subconsciously sought out other abusive situations—ones that confirmed his worthlessness, but also ones that he could endure. He attached to relationships and jobs that reinforced his feeling of not being good enough. The more he tried to please people, the more his shame was reinforced. His behaviors centered around keeping his abusers happy. Michael was living in a survival pattern at best.

He shared a phrase with me that he had learned in a PTSD support group: Abusers teach you how to abuse yourself. And unknowingly, that's what Michael had been doing most of his life.

After he married his wife, Michael began looking for work. With his high-tech smarts and good looks, he landed a job at a large media company. It was there that he met a coworker whose friendship changed his life. His friend, Adam, recognized Michael's talent and skills. Adam laughed at Michael's jokes and took Michael out for karaoke one night after work. Michael loved it. They started doing normal things in the world and Michael developed trust in someone for the first time. Prior to meeting his new friend at work Michael believed that the only way to get people to love him was to give everything away. He gave away his pride, his will, and his dreams. To experience care and positive attention was a revelation to Michael. This friendship was the first step to his healing.

Aware of Michael's history and self-defeating behavior, Adam spoke out about the abuse he saw in Michael's life. He was appalled at how Michael's wife and her family treated him, and Adam encouraged Michael to leave. Adam learned of the wife's controlling and manipulative father who was connected to the Mafia. The father strong-armed Michael to do what was in the "best interest" of the family always and to submit to his wife. Michael's wife gave him a meager weekly allowance for food and travel. It was less than a child's lunch money. Michael didn't realize anything was wrong with this due to his upbringing. She criticized everything about him, such as his laugh, his talents, and his intellect. It seemed her goal was to make fun of others with negative humor, like her Mafioso father. Michael couldn't take it any longer.

As Michael withdrew from his wife, he began to feel a new kind of anxiety. As his relationship was ending, so were the abuse and control. This broke the only pattern Michael had known. He didn't know how to function as a free person. The new anxiety became a problem on the job as he lashed out at coworkers. Eventually Michael was fired, but losing his job revealed a silver lining.

Within days Michael was hired over the phone for a new job. It thrilled him to learn that his resume was better than he thought, and his skills and abilities were of high value in his field. To be hired over the phone confirmed that it wasn't just his pretty-boy looks that allowed him to survive or succeed in the world. In his new job he found even more people who appreciated his talents and his personality. Michael was gaining confidence.

With a growing confidence, Michael knew that he needed to find safety and tranquility or he would lose himself completely. He decided that if he could walk away from his abusive marriage once and for all, he might have a chance of experiencing peace. Ultimately he hoped to die in God's graces, not within the abusive confines of his current hell.

When Michael left his wife, he left behind his clothes, five laptops containing his work portfolio, and all his possessions. With the loss of his wife and children, Michael lost everything he had, except his Soul.

This was not an easy move, given his wife's father was connected to the Mafia. For months, he feared for his life. Michael feels confident that regardless of the financial hardship and fear, it felt right to leave his wife. Having his Soul was his most important asset.

Michael started a new life in another state and began to repair his spirit. With meditation classes, support groups, PTSD therapy, and extensive emotional healing, Michael found his life, his voice, and his happiness. As a grown man, he has discovered self-will and that life is about more than survival. He learned how to set boundaries by saying no to employers and friends when appropriate and, in doing so, people still accepted him. He's realized that the world can be kind and as equally full of freedom and beauty as it is pain and suffering. Michael became awakened to worthiness, self-love, and compassion. Peace and clarity become more real to Michael each day as he stays present in the moment, owns his emotions, and travels the path of his Soul. This is enlightenment.

Spiritual awakening and enlightenment are not acquired at one point in time. Like healing, enlightenment a process. It isn't about chasing a goal or judging our experiences. There is no rite of passage. Awakening and enlightenment are powerful, yet personal, experiences that happen as the heart aligns with the Soul. This happens through the mindful practice of emotional healing.

The mind can create a world of illusions and it's important to not attach to these false promises of the world. Freedom and happiness come from within. You become closer to your truth by honoring your experiences and using the energy to fortify your life. It is the suffering that makes healing possible. Take the time and energy needed to process and attend to your feelings. Bow with humility to the wonder of life and divine order of all things. You don't become strong despite hardships, you become strong because of them. This is courage, love, and compassion rising. This is enlightenment, this is peace.

Crown Chakra Basics

Color: White or Violet

Gemstones: Amethyst, Clear Quartz, Selenite, Diamond, Celestite, Kyanite

Essential Oils: Frankincense, Lavender, Vetiver, Myrrh, Rosewood, Neroli, Palo Santo, Sandalwood, Cedarwood, Cypress, Eucalyptus

Meditation

Find a comfortable position and close your eyes. Bring your focus to the tip of your nose and notice the cool air flowing in on the inhale. Then notice the warm air flowing out on the exhale. Breathing should be effortless and free. As you inhale and exhale, repeat the mantra "I am light." On the inhale say to yourself "I am" and on the exhale "Light." Breathe like this for several rounds. Don't increase your breath; use regular gentle breathing. On your next inhale, visualize that your body is gently rising, as if in a hot-air balloon. Each inhale takes you up higher, and as you exhale, you maintain your position in a relaxed and peaceful way, like you are floating. Inhale up, exhale steady, and float. Imagine that your hot-air balloon takes you up among the clouds. You have no fear, only peace and connection with nature. You feel one with the universe. Inhale and imagine that you rise higher. You are light and weightless, without pain or worry. Your perspective broadens as you look out over the vastness around you. Eventually you will rise so high you can see the whole continent and its waters. You also see the Earth. Breathe and repeat the mantra "I am Light." Go as high as you feel comfortable and stay there for a few breaths, looking and appreciating the beauty from which you came. Allow your mind to open. Be at peace. When you are ready to exit the meditation, gently float down on each exhale. Slowly return to your body, using your senses to bring your awareness back to the room. Allow enough time to recalibrate into the present, and on the next inhale, gently open your eyes.

CONCLUSION

We are all just walking each other home.
—Ram Dass

Through time we acquire plenty of warts, imperfections, and scars. Through every event of my life, I have found that healing and happiness were possible if I stayed present to the emotion and not only accepted, but incorporated the experience into my life. Peace did not find me. I had to work to reconnect with my Soul. It is challenging to stay present to life within the turbulent confines of pain and suffering, but I did it and you can, too. It is truly the path to healing.

Each experience in your life is part of your spiritual evolution. At times there seems to be no reason or justification for the sorrow and pain we endure. I do not believe God's will is to hurt or harm us, but to allow us to experience the fullness of our glory. We must travel the roads of grief and suffering before reaching the heights of love and compassion. We can turn away from the events that take us to the edge, or we can honor God's gifts that encourage our transcendence.

My wish is for this book to inspire and empower you to explore your depth and express your authentic self. The pathway of your heart is the route to healing. It takes courage to stay with the healing process, to risk love, to take responsibility for your happiness, and to embrace your past. Feel proud and encouraged that you seek the highest good for yourself. This is the epitome of self-love.

The core principles of connection, acceptance, and Spiritual Mapping can be used time and again as you move through life and experience the next struggle. It is through the emotional process that you can walk through fear into action and peace. Remember: Healing is a continual journey. It's a process, not a finish line.

Life is not easy but it becomes more meaningful as we discover our true nature and live authentically. Strive to become the pillar of strength, not a defender of negative thoughts or energy. Do not listen to the false illusions of fear that the mind creates. Your Soul is your essence. Follow its guidance and honor your heart and there you will find freedom. Take action through the moments of struggle and give your feelings attention. Each breath and movement can be a step toward emotional wellness.

You are not weak, nor should you cower in defense of fear. You were made with power and love. Weakness comes from separating yourself from your Soul. We do this by believing the false ideas of the mind or the negative input of others in our environment. As we walk with intention of healing and happiness, it is important to stay connected to our inner wisdom and to expect guidance from Source. We need to listen to our hearts, our souls, and our inner wisdom to experience the life we desire. Connection brings healing and wholeness. Disconnection leads to fragmented thinking, fear, anxiety, and disillusion. The beauty of life is that you have an opportunity at any moment to build a new foundation, regardless of your age, income, or life situation.

Understanding the difference between divine direction and wishful thinking can be difficult. I believe we miss many miracles and magic in life due to the blocks of the mind and the heart.

I hope that you can begin opening to the mystical possibilities of divine direction. I, too, have had to step out in faith to follow the call of my spirit and what felt like the call of a higher power. I have a passion to help others, but that was not the only impetus to write this book. I was directed to do it by communication that is hard to explain. A voice spoke to me, first in a dream, and then later, during a meditation. No matter how much I resisted, the messages were impossible to ignore. As I teetered on the direction my work should take, I was motivated by the messages and the encouragement of others to put my thoughts to paper.

One night I heard a voice as I slept. It was a dream, but it was absent of any visual framework. It was just the darkness behind my eyelids and an audible, clear voice. The voice sounded androgynous; otherwise there was nothing unusual about it. I had never heard voices before but it said, "You are to continue the work of John Lennon." I responded in the dream by saying, "You mean of peace and love?" And the voice said, "Beyond." I snapped awake and wondered what that was all about. It was a very strange event.

The dream message caught me off guard. I had no connection to John Lennon, nor did I have a goal to extend his message of peace to the world. I put the dream out of my mind and moved forward in my work with the vague notion that someday I might write a book on healing.

It was at least six months later that I began to develop this book proposal. I discovered I was referencing self-love and peace as a by-product of emotional healing, so much so that it became part of the subtitle. One afternoon I was writing while sitting in my rock garden facing the skyline of New York City. Suddenly the John Lennon dream came flashing back to me. I smiled as I realized the connection of my writing to the larger scope of the peace movement. I felt I was carrying forth the energy of peace, albeit in a different way.

Several months later, I attended a meditation in Manhattan. I meditated while sitting on a cushion in a big room filled with silence and strangers. It was not a guided class, just an open sit to allow people to come and go on their own schedule. Unless I am teaching meditation or at Modern Sage in a group, I usually prefer to practice at home, but this evening I felt an urge to have a new experience. Less than five minutes into the meditation I heard a voice. It was as clear as someone sitting next to me. The voice was different from the one in the dream although it was also androgynous in tone, yet more assertive in its message. The words were so audible that I couldn't believe my ears. I was compelled to preserve the message so I gingerly pulled out my phone and wrote verbatim what the voice said. It was like an intercom message from another dimension with specific information about my life.

Essentially, the voice said that I am a living spirit guide and I am here to help people heal and confront their true selves. It confirmed that my personal trials were preparing and strengthening me to support the masses. My courage to stand before people and share my stories allows others to better understand themselves. The message warned that some people may not like my work and will turn away, but I should understand and accept their response. It encouraged me to continue to be present and help those who want access to their healing. The voice also told me to be as open and clear as possible and incorporate this divine guidance in my words.

I still do not know where this voice came from but I jumped off that cushion to go share this experience with my friends. That message lit a fire in my belly and I had a new eagerness to write this book. It seemed part of my calling.

I'm grateful for the guidance of the voice. It helped me be fearless on my path to healing by helping others awaken to theirs. No longer do I need to hide behind my fear, but put to good use the voice and wisdom from my personal life experiences and thoughtful study.

I believe we all serve as living spirit guides. There is a voice giving a message and guidance to each of us. It's your call, your charge, and your purpose. To reveal that purpose, you must be free from the binds of emotional suffering, and accept and honor the experiences that have been offered.

We are here with a purpose and mission to learn how to love, guide, and uplift each other on the journey back home. To be present and available promotes personal growth and it allows us to genuinely help others. Emotional healing not only serves you, it serves your neighbor, your friends, and your families. People we love often need us to be examples and encouragement for their own healing. I believe it's an honor and responsibility to partake in the guidance of others, and it should inspire us to continue our own self-development.

Life never stays the same. It either decomposes and transforms, or grows and transcends. Our bodies decline in age and will eventually feed the energy of the next life. Our hearts, though, can continue to blossom and evolve until we meet the truest nature of our souls. Part of awakening and enlightenment is the realization of this higher purpose, and there is nothing greater than to walk the path with others in alignment with love.

I encourage you to stay close to the process of healing. The commitment to self and Soul is worth it. The benefits are real and tangible. Do not sit idle in the stagnant energy of apathy waiting for the dark cloud to lift. Get involved and be active in your healing. Peace is not passive. It takes commitment to stay aligned with your Soul, it takes acceptance to keep your heart open, and it takes trust to transcend the fears of your mind into freedom. As you practice, you will awaken to self-love and inner peace.

God bless you on your journey. Much love.

INDEX

Abandonment, 28
    fear of, 20
Abuse, 31, 59
Acceptance, 41-44, 46, 208
Action, 66, 82, 96
Addiction, 29, 82, 140, 186
Aggression, 82
Alignment, 184
Allowing emotion, 127
Altered state of consciousness, 34
Amnesia, emotional, 116
Anger, 39, 139, 186
Anxiety, 15, 26, 27, 28, 29, 31, 47,
    54, 112, 139, 145, 162-166, 177
Apathy, 112, 187
Aromatherapy, 179
Arrogance, 137
Attachment, 36, 47-48
Attention, seeking, 138
Authentic living, 28
Authenticity, 66, 83, 88, 91-92,
    127, 136, 143, 145, 147, 208
Avoidance, 29

Awakening, 195-204
Awareness, 168, 185
Balance Nutrition, 47
Balance, 14, 29-35, 47, 90, 136
Barricades, emotional, 62
Behavior, negative, 85
Beliefs, 188
    spiritual, 194-195
Blame, 145
Blamers, 48-49
Blocked energy, 54-55
Boundaries, 98
Brain, the, 157-158, 160-161
Bravery, 17
Breath, healing and, 165-167
Bridges, 122-123
Brow Chakra, 161-162, 180
Bullies, 142
Capabilities, 79
Care-tending, 47
Change, 108
Chanting, 148
Character, flawless, 196

Children, 72, 78, 80, 138, 142, 168, 178, 186

Circumstance, 62

Clouds, 108-110

Co-dependency, 31, 60

Color therapy, 20

Communication, 133-134, 151

Compassion, 113, 188, 196, 207

Complaining, 29

Confidence, 82, 113, 136, 149

Connection from Source, 29

Connection, 33, 36, 40, 83, 128, 208

Connectivity, 15

Conscious thought, 157-161

Consciousness, 72
    altered state of, 34

Constant worry, 163-164

Control issues, 29

Control, 82, 96, 99-101, 134, 159

Core, 55, 100

Courage, 121, 208

Creativity, 52, 70-71, 73, 150

Creator, 192-193

Crown Chakra, 185, 194, 204

Cycle, the healing, 127

Dance, 75

Death, 108, 187

Deceit, 136, 137, 140

Deep listening, 152

Defense position, 96-97

Denial, 42-43, 62, 111

Depletion, 97

Depression, 15, 26, 27, 31, 112, 162, 164, 186

Despair, 26

Detachment, 15, 16, 34, 35, 36, 48, 85

Digestion, 55

Disappointment, 29

Disassociation, 16

Disconnection, 16, 35, 108, 111, 141, 208

Disconnections from the Soul, 61

Dis-ease, emotional, 28

Dismissing emotion, 128

Displacement, 16

Dissatisfaction, 29

Distractions, 66, 167-168

Divine direction, 209

Eating disorders, 18, 29, 82

Ego, 39

Embarrassment, 136, 140

Emotion,
    allowing, 127
    dismissing, 128
    expressing, 142-143

Emotional
    amnesia, 116
    barricades, 62
    dis-ease, 28
    energies, 67-70, 110
    entrapment, 16
    healing, 12, 14-17, 44, 86-87, 111, 183, 211
    imbalance, 133
    injuries, 62-63
    stagnation, 55

Emotions of suffering, 52

Emotions, 159
    essential, 35
    hiding, 78
    negative, 60, 79, 114,
        139, 164
    processing, 56, 61
    repressed, 162-163
    underlying, 166
    unprocessed, 18
    unresolved, 162
Empathy, 151-152
Energetic imbalance, 56
Energies,
    emotional, 67-70
    imbalanced, 18
Energy
    healing, 90
    imbalances, 82
    medicine, 13
    vampires, 96-97
Energy, 18
    blocked, 54-55
    emotional, 110
    negative, 208
Enlightenment, 178, 184, 185,
    195-204
Envy, 112
Equanimity, 44
Essential emotions, 35
Estrangement, 114
Events, pivotal, 11
Excuses, 29, 149
Exhaustion, 97
Experiences, life, 11-12
Expression, the power of, 134

False identity, 146
Familiarity, 171
Fatigue, 112
Fault, 114
Fear, 15, 26, 27, 31, 38, 39, 41, 65,
    73, 82, 89, 107-108, 127-128,
    145, 159, 160, 162, 163, 164,
    183, 198
    being human and, 27-29
Feeling Center, 55, 58, 59, 70, 74,
    75, 83
Feeling, thinking vs., 122
Feelings, triggers vs., 444-6
Feet to Earth Grounding
    Exercise, 34
Flawless character, 196
Flexibility, 57
Focus, 177
Following your heart, 119-122
Forgiveness, 196
Fragmentation, 15
Frame of reference, 151
Freedom, 73, 77, 119, 146, 185,
    203-204
Frustration, 187
Gardening, 48
Gemstones, 20
God, 184, 187, 193
Grace, 119
Grasping, 40-41
Gravity, 30
Grief, 26, 28, 39, 62, 115-119,
    145, 150, 183, 207
Groundedness, 30-31, 47-48
Grudges, 112

Guidance, spiritual, 187-190
Guilt, 39, 57-64, 150, 183, 187
Gut, the, 67, 69
Habits, 87
    negative, 79
Happiness, 17, 26, 27, 28, 33, 44,
    47, 115-116, 184, 196, 203-
    204, 207
Healing cycle, the, 127
Healing Touch, 90
Healing, 12-14, 27, 43-46, 52, 55,
    63-64, 79, 110, 118-119, 230,
    207, 208
    breath and, 165-167
    emotional, 12, 14-17, 44,
        86-87, 111, 211
    energy, 90
Health, your voice and your, 133
Healthy
    control, 100
    shame, 90-92
Heart Chakra, 111-113, 118, 128
Heart,
    following your, 119-122
    living from the, 38
    traveling your, 122-123
Heartache, 38
Help, 99
Heroes, 33-34
Hiding your emotions, 78
Hiding, 94-95
Higher Power, 192-193
Hoarseness, 133
Honesty, 19

Hope, 15, 26
Humanness, 15
    Soul vs. 13
Identity, 77-78
    false, 146
Illusion, 184, 203-204
Imagination, 70
Imbalance, 18, 57, 162, 163, 165
    emotional, 133
    energetic, 56
    physical, 56
Imbalanced energies, 18, 82
Imperfection, 147
Indecision, 162
Injuries, emotional, 62-63
Injustice, 39
Inner peace, 38, 211
Inner wisdom, 159, 161
Insecurity, 31
Insomnia, 186
Inspiration, 26
Integrity, 136
Intimacy, 52, 73, 94
Intuition, 13, 161, 168-173, 196
Invisible cloak of protection, 28
Irrational fear, 160
Isolation, 29, 112, 187
Jealousy, 29, 112
Journaling, 173
Joy, 187
Judgment, 81, 137, 158, 178
Laziness, 87
Letting go, 35
Lies, 136, 137-141, 183

Life experiences, 11-12, 18

Listening, 66, 151-152

    deep, 152

Living from the heart, 38

Living, authentic, 28

Loneliness, 20, 28, 187

Love, 28, 33, 39-40, 62, 65, 89, 107, 112, 114-115, 116, 128, 187, 207

Maharaj, Nisargadatta, 91

Manipulation, 136, 137

Mediocrity, 39

Meditation, 13, 19, 31, 55, 159, 177-180, 188, 192-195

Memories, 45

Mindfulness, 55, 157-161

Mindlessness, 157

Mini Vipassana, 152

Mission, 211

Mood swings, 47

Moodiness, 112

Morals, 90

Movement, 133

Music, 75

Negative

    behavior, 85

    emotions, 60, 79, 114, 139, 164

    energy, 208

    habits, 79

    patterning, 87

    thinking, 136

Obesity, 18

Objectification, 72-73

OCD, 18, 29, 162

Openness, 74

Originality, 147

Over-controlling, 99

Pain, 52, 107, 138, 141, 207

Panic, 29

Passion, 51-52

Patience, 151

Patterning, negative, 87

Peace, 77, 184, 187, 190-191, 19, 207, 211

Perfection, 198

Perfectionism, 29

Performance anxiety, 150

Personal boundaries, 98

Personality, 78

Perspective of fear, 108

Perspective, 19, 151

Phobias, 28, 114, 162

Physical

    healing, 12

    imbalance, 56

Physicality, 46-48

Pillar of strength, 37-38, 55, 208

Pivotal events, 11

Polarity of thought, 160

Polarity Therapy, 90

Post Traumatic Emotional Disorder (PTED), 16-17, 110

Potential, 85

Power of expression, the, 134

Power of your will, 101-102

Power position, 96-97

Power, 82

Prayer, 188, 192-195

Presence, 32

Processing emotions, 61
　　women and, 56

Protection, 96-98, 138
　　invisible cloak of, 28

Purity, 197

Purpose, 79, 87, 211

Rational fear, 160

Reality, detachment from, 34

Rectification, 90-91

Redemption, 15, 26

Reference, frame of, 151

Reiki, 200

Relationships, 71-75

Remorse, 28

Replaying trauma, 46

Repressed emotions, 162-163

Resentment, 186

Responsibility, 17, 145, 208

Restriction, 133

Root Chakra, 29-35, 48,49,
　　55, 159

Routines, 87

Sacral Chakra, 54-57, 74, 75,
　　83, 159

Seat of Emotion, 136

Secrets, 141

Seeking attention, 138

Self, 15, 33, 54
　　true, 77

Self-care, 111, 177

Self-control, 82, 99

Self-discovery, 94

Self-doubt, 29, 136

Self-expression, 147-150

Self-harm, 78, 82

Self-love, 47, 55, 64, 113, 184,
　　195-196, 211

Self-shaming, 48

Self-talk, negative, 29

Self-trust, 113

Self-will, 77

Self-worth, 26, 83, 162

Senses, 159

Separation, 35, 93

Service to others, 113

Sex, 71-75

Sexualization, 72-73

Shame, 15, 39, 44, 60, 78, 79,
　　80-92, 93, 136, 138, 140,
　　150, 162, 183, 187

Shame, healthy, 90-92

Shamers, 48-49

Sharing, 83

Shock, 62

Shyness, 29, 137

Sickness, 62

Sixth sense, 168

Skin conditions, 28

Sleeplessness, 28

Solar Plexus Chakra, 78-80,
　　81-83, 102, 159

Sorrow, 107, 207

Soul Signs, 49

Soul, 15, 27, 39, 44, 45, 48, 62,
　　70, 71, 77, 79, 87, 88, 108,
　　123, 147, 184-185, 188, 190,
　　195, 207

Soul, disconnection from the, 61

Soul, humanness vs., 13
Soul, spirit vs., 64-67
Sound vibration, 58
Sound, 133
Source, connection from, 29
Speaking your truth, 145-147
Spirit guides, 211
Spirit, Soul vs., 64-67
Spiritual
    awakening, 195
    beliefs, 194-195
    enlightenment, 178
    guidance, 187-190
Spiritual Mapping, 19-20, 173, 208
Spiritual work, 188
Stability, 31
Stagnation, emotional, 55
Strength, pillar of, 208
Stress hormones, 160
Stress, 28, 165, 187
Stubbornness, 137
Suffering, 39, 44, 51-52, 55,
    63-64, 108, 111, 138, 142,
    183, 187, 207
Suffering, the emotions of, 52
Tattle-tales, 138
Thinking,
    feeling vs., 122
    negative, 136
    wishful, 209
Third Eye, 161, 168
Thought, polarity of, 160
Thoughts, negative, 208
Throat Chakra, 136-137, 150, 153
Tranquility, 44

Trauma, 38, 39, 46, 110
Traveling your heart, 122-123
Triggers, feelings vs., 44-46
True self, 77
Trust, 33, 66, 101, 185
Trusted Nurturer, 74
Truth, 136, 137-14
    being human and, 27-29
    speaking your, 145-147
Underlying emotions, 166
Unevenness, 133
Unknown, the, 163
Unprocessed emotions, 18
Unprocessed grief, 115
Unresolved emotions, 162
Values, 90
Victims, 49, 145-146
Violation, 114
Vipassana, mini, 152
Vision board, 71
Visualization, 176
Voice, 133-136, 151
Vulnerability, 74, 128
Weakness, 27, 133, 208
Wellness, 14
Wholeness, 15, 44
Will, power of your, 101-102
Willpower, 29, 78
Wisdom, 187, 197
    inner, 161
Wishful thinking, 209
Worry, constant, 163-164
Worth, 118
Writing, 66, 173
Yoga, 188

ABOUT THE AUTHOR

Leah Guy is an intuitive transpersonal healer, spiritual teacher, professional speaker, and media personality. She has developed a framework to help people transform trauma and pain into peace and wholeness. Using her personal triumphs in addition to more than two decades of working with clients, she has helped people move from fear and disconnection to heart-centered and peaceful living. She is a sought-after inspirational speaker who has appeared on major media outlets as an expert on topics such as meditation, the mind-body connection, energy medicine and chakra balancing, intuition, and addiction, as well as emotional and spiritual healing. Her down-to-earth, honest, and often-humorous approach makes her one of the most accessible leaders in the field. Known as The Modern Sage, she is the owner of two companies: Modern Sage, LLC, and A Girl Named Guy Productions, LLC, a lifestyle media company. If you would like to invite Leah for a speaking engagement or workshop, please inquire at Media@ModernSage.com. To inquire about private sessions with Leah or other qualified colleagues that she recommends, please call (201) 360-2318. Leah resides in Jersey City, New Jersey. For more information, visit her online at ModernSage.com or across social media channels @TheModernSage.

MORE INFORMATION

If you would like more information on concepts found in this book or supportive products, go to *www.ModernSage.com*. You will find recommended reading that will expand your knowledge on the energy system, intuition, holistic living, and mindfulness. You will also find supportive healing items including spiritual and personal care products, gemstones, and gifts. Tutorials and additional teaching materials are offered regularly. Please sign up for the newsletter to receive bi-weekly inspirations, meditations, and notices.

I am also on social media and love to interact! You can find me under the names @TheModernSage or Leah Guy. I frequently post how-to videos, photos, mantras, and notices about my teachings and workshop offerings.

At Modern Sage's healing center, we offer weekly workshops and classes, bodywork services, and natural and holistic products and gifts, as well as metaphysical items. Please visit us if you are in the New York City area!